HEALTH CARE IN TRANSITION

PRIVATE-SECTOR HEALTH INSURANCE

A PRIMER

HEALTH CARE IN TRANSITION

Additional books in this series can be found on Nova's website under the Series tab.

Additional e-books in this series can be found on Nova's website under the e-book tab.

HEALTH CARE IN TRANSITION

PRIVATE-SECTOR HEALTH INSURANCE

A PRIMER

STEPHEN MAXWELL MATHIS
EDITOR

nova publishers
New York

Library of Congress Cataloging-in-Publication Data

ISBN: 978-1-63483-772-9

Published by Nova Science Publishers, Inc. † New York

CONTENTS

PREFACE

Congress has seen a renewed interest in the market for private health insurance since the passage of the Patient Protection and Affordable Care Act (ACA). This book provides an overview of private-sector (as opposed to government-provided) health insurance. It serves as an introduction to health insurance from the point of view of many consumers under the age of 65. Furthermore, the book provides background information about modifying or building on the current health insurance system; discusses how understanding the potential impact of such proposals requires a working knowledge of how health insurance is provided, purchased, and regulated; and describes various ACA provisions that affect the private insurance market.

In: Private-Sector Health Insurance
Editor: Stephen Maxwell Mathis

ISBN: 978-1-63483-772-9

Chapter 1

AN INTRODUCTION TO HEALTH INSURANCE: WHAT SHOULD A CONSUMER KNOW?*

Carol Rapaport

SUMMARY

Congress has seen a renewed interest in the market for private health insurance since the passage of the Patient Protection and Affordable Care Act (ACA; P.L. 111-148, as amended). This report provides an overview of private-sector (as opposed to government-provided) health insurance. It serves as an introduction to health insurance from the point of view of many consumers under the age of 65. No background in health insurance is assumed, and all terms are defined in the body of the report.

A consumer may find the purchase of health care inherently different from some other purchases. Health care can be expensive, and many relevant details concerning future health care may not be known when the consumer is choosing an insurance plan, including when over the course of a year (if at all) health care will be purchased, which services will be needed, and the costs of those services. These characteristics of purchasing health care decrease the consumer's ability to plan financially and increase the consumer's exposure to financial risk. The purchase of

* This is an edited, reformatted and augmented version of a Congressional Research Service publication R44014, prepared for Members and Committees of Congress, dated April 30, 2015.

health insurance reduces the risks and unpredictability inherent in paying for health services.

An employed consumer may obtain health insurance from his or her employer if health insurance is offered by the employer (known as employer-sponsored insurance, or ESI) as a fringe benefit. All consumers may purchase health insurance directly (perhaps through an insurance agent or broker) from private insurance firms. In addition, all consumers may obtain health insurance through insurance exchanges, or marketplaces. Exchanges facilitate transactions between buyers and sellers of insurance but are not insurers.

Health insurance plans can differ across many dimensions, including coverage, costs, flexibility in choosing providers, special features, and generosity. Two specific health insurance plan types that may be of interest to Congress are consumer-directed health care (CDHC) and value-based insurance design (VBID). Both these plan types have the potential to lower aggregate health care (however measured) by providing incentives for consumers to seek less care, or less expensive care.

Which particular health insurance plan a consumer chooses depends on a number of factors, including the expected health of those covered by the plan, the price of the plan and of the medical services it provides, the consumer's income, and the prices of the other goods and services the consumer wishes to purchase. In addition, because some health insurance plans are tied to employment, the consumer's status as an employee also influences (and is influenced by) his or her choice of health insurance.

INTRODUCTION

Congress has seen a renewed interest in questions related to the market for private health insurance since the passage of the Patient Protection and Affordable Care Act (ACA; P.L. 111- 148, as amended). Recent health insurance marketplace changes include a different way to purchase health insurance (exchanges) and a new system of categorizing the generosity of plans' health coverage based on the names of various metals (e.g., bronze and silver).[1] Some consumers may face different choices of health insurance plans than in the past. Not all consumers are comfortable with the various concepts governing which health insurance plan might be best for them.

This report provides an overview of private-sector (as opposed to government-provided) health insurance. It serves as an introduction to health insurance from the point of view of consumers under the age of 65 who purchase a health insurance plan.[2] No background in health insurance is assumed, and all terms are defined. The report therefore can be viewed as an introduction to the more comprehensive discussion of health insurance found in the Congressional Research Service (CRS) health insurance primer.[3]

WHAT IS HEALTH INSURANCE?

This section of the report covers the differences between a consumer's purchase of health care and his or her purchase of other goods and services. For example, budgeting for health care expenses may be more difficult than budgeting for other services. The purchase of health insurance reduces the risks and unpredictability inherent in a consumer's health care expenses. The consumer pays for a health insurance policy and then is subsequently (partly) reimbursed for his or her future expenditures on health care.[4]

The Challenges of Purchasing Health Care

A consumer may find the purchase of health care different from some other purchases. For example, a consumer buying a gallon of milk each week often knows in advance what kind of milk he or she wants and the approximate price of each variety of milk. In addition, expenditures on milk are rarely an especially high proportion of the consumer's monthly spending.

The consumer's decision to purchase health care, however, is more complicated. Health care can be expensive, especially for major illnesses or injuries. In addition, the consumer may not know in advance when (if at all) over the course of a year he or she will purchase the health services, what services he or she will need, and how much the services will cost. Each of these characteristics of health care decreases the consumer's ability to plan financially and increases the exposure to financial risk.

Few other goods and services have these characteristics. When a consumer thinks about other large expenditures, four years of college might come to mind. However, the potential students and their parents know when college expenses will become due well in advance of the due date. It is much easier to predict that Junior will need $20,000 in August 2015 to pay freshman tuition than that Junior will need $5,000 to pay for health care after he breaks his leg skiing over winter break.

Health care also may differ from other types of unpredictable expenditures. If a consumer were unexpectedly invited to a black-tie event, she may decide to purchase a gown. Even though this purchase was unpredictable, the cost of the gown often is a much smaller percentage of her monthly income than the cost of most medical treatments. Finally, consumers are likely to know what types of gowns (and milk) they prefer. They may be less clear whether they need a cast or a splint to repair their injured ankle. Consumers therefore are more likely to rely on their doctors' opinions when using health care than on their grocery clerks' opinions when buying milk. All these features increase the financial riskiness and unpredictability associated with using health care.

Health Insurance Can Help Consumers Manage Risk

The purchase of health insurance reduces the risks and unpredictability inherent in a consumer's cost of health care. Typically, a consumer selects a particular health insurance plan just before the start of the health insurance plan year and then pays a monthly premium to the health insurer.[5] In return, if the consumer receives health care over the course of the year, the health insurer may pay some (or all) of the costs, depending on the details of the plan. For example, if the consumer does use health care, he or she often has to pay something out of his or her own pocket. The level of out-of-pocket (OOP) expenses varies across health insurance plans. Although health insurance may never make health care free of charge for the consumer, it often results in lower OOP expenses, especially when evaluated over the entire term of the plan.[6]

Not all holders of health insurance end up using health care over the year. However, when considered over a multiyear period, health insurance may help a consumer manage the risk associated with a large potential financial loss from health care costs.[7]

Consumers also may buy health insurance because they may be required either to maintain health insurance coverage or pay a penalty. In other words, many consumers face a *mandate* to be insured.[8]

How Can a Consumer Purchase Health Insurance?

A consumer may obtain health insurance from an employer (or other group) or individually from another source.

From an Employer or Other Group

Some consumers obtain health insurance plans offered by employers to their employees and their employees' dependents as fringe benefits.[9] When employees obtain health insurance through their employer, the cost of the health insurance plan often is shared between the employee and the employer.[10] In addition, other groups whose members share a common bond, such as labor unions and some other associations, can offer members an opportunity to purchase health insurance through the group.

If an employee purchases insurance offered through his or her employer (employer-sponsored insurance, or ESI), the employee enrolls in a plan through the employer without interacting with salespeople and other representatives of health insurers. ESI is therefore relatively easy to obtain. If an employee does not want to accept an offer of group insurance, he or she is free to purchase health insurance from another source.

When a consumer with ESI leaves his or her place of employment for any reason, that consumer may lose health insurance. Those who retire any time after reaching the age of 65 usually will be eligible for Medicare, the federal health insurance entitlement program for those with disabilities and those aged 65 and older.[11] Consumers terminated from employment without cause generally are eligible for COBRA, a federal program through which certain terminated consumers may continue to receive their ESI for a period of time as long as they pay the total cost of the insurance plan.[12] Consumers also may be eligible for other federal and state health insurance programs or can choose to purchase private insurance that is not from a group.

Not from a Group

Consumers who are not offered or who do not purchase group insurance may use insurance brokers and agents, including web-based brokers, to learn about health insurance plans.[13] Brokers and agents are licensed by the states and generally are paid on commission by insurers. Agents work with one insurer, whereas brokers can work with more than one insurer.

Consumers may purchase health insurance policies either directly from insurers (perhaps represented by brokers and agents) or from exchanges, which sell the insurers' plans. Insurance exchanges serve as marketplaces for health insurance plans in that they facilitate transactions between the buyers of insurance (consumers) and sellers of insurance (insurers). In general, consumers must use exchanges in their states of residence.[14]

How Do Health Insurance Plans Differ?

Health insurance plans can differ in terms of their coverage of consumers and services, their costs to the consumers (and consumers' dependents or employers, if relevant), special features, and generosity, among other properties.

By Coverage

Covered Individuals

The consumer may buy a health insurance plan covering one person, a family, or other groupings. Under self-only coverage, the consumer is the only person insured. Family coverage applies to the consumer and any spouse and/or dependents. Other possibilities include self plus one and self plus children.[15]

If their parent's health insurance plan covers children, children can be added to their parent's plan until they turn 26 years of age. Those children under the age of 26 can join or remain on their parent's plan even if they are married, not living with a parent, attending school, not financially dependent on a parent, or eligible to enroll in their own employer's plan.

Many consumers with ESI obtain and renew their employer's plan during open enrollment season. During *open season*, consumers can change health insurance policies. Outside of open season, consumers cannot change their health insurance plan unless they experience a qualifying life event. *Qualifying life events* include marriage, moving to a new state, divorce, and childbirth. Open season in the exchanges is similar to open season in ESI.

Covered Services

A consumer might use a variety of health care services over the course of the year. Office visits to a health care provider may include routine well-adult exams, nonroutine flu care, and urgent treatment for bone breaks.[16] The consumer might require X-rays and laboratory tests at some visits. More serious matters may require treatment at a hospital. Some consumers may need medical equipment, others may need a recovery program for substance abuse, and still others may find a single prescription treatment sufficient.

Given the breadth of possible health care, a consumer probably will not find a health insurance plan that covers all possible care. For example, almost no policies cover health care that is not deemed medically necessary by the insurer. *Medically necessary care* is "needed to prevent, diagnose or treat an illness, injury, condition, disease or its symptoms and that meet accepted standards of medicine."[17] For example, reconstructive breast surgery following a mastectomy performed as part of breast cancer treatment is medically necessary (as well as required by law).[18] In addition, health insurance generally covers breast augmentation to correct a congenital defect in breast development. However, it generally does not cover breast augmentation for cosmetic purposes. Not all insurers consider the same medical goods and services to be medically necessary.

Even among services widely agreed to be medically necessary among insurers, consumers will find that not all health insurance plans cover the same health services. In addition, the specifics of the covered service may differ across plans. For example, plans may differ across coverage of the number of routine maternal visits and the conditions under which a caesarean section is a covered service. Similarly, the consumer may choose among plans that cover eating disorder treatments differently.

By Costs

Premiums

Consumers pay *premiums*, which are the prices of private health insurance plan coverage for a given period of time. Premiums are owed whether or not the consumer actually seeks health care during the time covered by the plan. Consumers who purchase insurance policies directly from insurers or through the exchanges (for individuals) almost always pay the entire amount of the premium themselves. Many consumers who purchase ESI share the premium cost with their employers. In other words, the consumer pays for part of the premium (generally through payroll deductions) and the employer pays for part of the premium (using funds that are not part of an individual's hourly wages or annual salary).[19]

Certain consumers who purchase health insurance through the exchanges may be eligible for *premium tax credits.* These credits reduce the price of the premium by returning part of its dollar value as a portion of the consumer's income tax refund. Eligibility for the tax credits depends on whether the consumer is eligible for various types of health insurance plans and on family income.[20]

Cost Sharing

Cost sharing refers to the part of the costs for health services covered by the insurance plan that is paid by the consumer (or the person responsible for the consumer's bills). Deductibles, coinsurance, and co-payments are examples of cost sharing.

A *deductible* is the amount of money an insured consumer may be required to pay the medical care providers OOP (over the term of the insurance policy) before receiving any benefits from the health insurance policy. In other words, the consumer must spend up to the deductible OOP on covered services before the health insurance plan will begin to pay its part of health costs for most covered health services. A consumer is therefore required to *meet the deductible* before the insurance plan contributes to the costs of his or her health care. *Preventive medical services* are certain covered services not subject to deductibles (or any other form of cost sharing) when received from in-network providers.[21] In addition, not all health insurance plans have a deductible, and plans may have different deductibles for different types of services.

The consumer may pay *coinsurance*, which is a percentage of the total amount billed to the consumer. For example, consider a consumer whose chest X-ray is billed at $150. A 20% coinsurance rate means that the consumer pays $30 and the insurer pays $120 (both to the provider) for the X-ray. These calculations assume that the consumer has met the deductible. If the deductible has not been met, the consumer must pay his or her bill in full until the deductible is met.

Alternatively, the consumer may pay a flat-rate *co-payment*. For example, a $20 co-payment for that chest X-ray would mean that the recipient must pay $20 to the provider OOP for the same X-ray, assuming the consumer's deductible has been met. The insurer would then pay $130 to the provider. Once again, if the deductible has not been met, the recipient must pay the amount remaining until the deductible is met.[22]

A consumer who requires a significant amount of health care may reach a high level of OOP spending. A maximum *OOP limit*, however, sets a cap on consumer spending. Once a consumer reaches the OOP spending limit, the insurer is responsible for all billed costs owed by the consumer for covered services from in-network providers.

Table 1. Comparison of Select Cost-Related Concepts, by Health Insurance

	ESI Purchased as Employer Fringe Benefit[a]	Individual Plan Purchased from Insurer	Individual Plan Purchased Through Exchange
Premium	Permitted	Permitted	Permitted
Premium Tax Credit	Not available	Not available	Available to those meeting income and other requirements[b]
Premium Contributions from Employer	Available, if offered by employer	Not available	Not available
Coverage of Preventive Health Services with No Cost Sharing	Required for in-network providers[c] in non-grandfathered plans[d]	Required for in-network providersc in non-grandfathered plans[d]	Required for in-network providersc in non-grandfathered plans[d]
Cost Sharing	Permitted	Permitted	Permitted
Cost-Sharing Subsidy	Not available	Not available	Available to those meeting income and other requirements[b]
Maximum Out-of-Pocket Limit	$6,600 for an individual plan and $13,200 for a family plan, unless the plan is grandfatheredd	$6,600 for an individual plan and $13,200 for a family plan, unless the plan is grandfatheredd	$6,600 for an individual plan and $13,200 for a family plan

Sources: CRS Report R42069, Private Health Insurance Market Reforms in the Affordable Care Act (ACA), by Annie L. Mach and Bernadette Fernandez. The source for the final row is https://www.healthcare.gov/glossary/out-ofpocket-maximum-limit/.

Notes:

[a] ESI stands for employer-sponsored insurance.

[b] The other requirements are whether the consumer is eligible for a government-sponsored health insurance plan, an ESI plan, a plan in the individual market, or a grandfathered plan.

[c] A network is a group of providers that have agreed to provide health care under specified terms to those consumers who have signed up for a particular insurance plan.

[d] Grandfathered health insurance plans are plans in which a consumer was enrolled on March 23, 2010, and that meet a few additional criteria.

Consumers who are eligible for premium tax credits through the exchanges also may be eligible for *cost-sharing subsides* through the exchanges. These subsidies reduce the costs associated with the use of covered services. As with the tax credit, eligibility for the cost-sharing subsidies depends on whether the consumer is eligible for various types of health insurance plans and on family income.

Select benefits of three representative health insurance policies are roughly characterized in *Table 1*. The plans are an ESI plan obtained as a fringe benefit from the consumer's employer, an individual insurance plan purchased directly by a consumer from an insurer, and an individual insurance plan purchased by a consumer through an exchange.

In summary, the consumers' costs differ in at least two respects. First, premium tax credits and cost-sharing subsidies are only available for plans purchased through an exchange (for individuals), and not through a private insurer or through ESI. Second, only consumers with ESI can have part of their premiums paid for by their employers.

By Networks and Flexibility in Choosing Providers

Before a consumer can use health care, he or she must decide from which providers to seek care. Some insurance plans do not provide financial incentives to influence the consumer's choice in any way. Other plans tie the provider that the consumer uses to the level of cost sharing the consumer faces. In particular, some consumers may want to use providers in their health plan network. A *network* is a group of providers that have agreed to provide health care under specified terms to those consumers who have signed up for a particular insurance plan. Many health plans decrease the consumer's cost-sharing obligations if they use in-network providers. It is thought that the health insurers can negotiate lower prices with their in-network providers. This is because the in-network providers are willing to accept lower prices because their pool of potential patients increases as the providers join the network. The in-network consumers then face lower cost sharing if they stay in-network. In contrast, in some cases, the consumer will owe 100% of the provider's bill for an out-of-network visit.[23]

Several broad categories of health plan types and their associated networks exist. The following plan descriptions are generalizations.[24] Health plan rules may differ from what is indicated; for example, a plan that usually does not cover health care received out-of-network often does cover such care when the only provider qualified to perform the care is out-of-network.

- Indemnity insurance allows the insured consumer to decide when and from whom to seek health care. There is no network of providers; a consumer may see any service provider and owe the level of cost sharing specified by the insurance plan. The consumer's indemnity insurance plan typically has some combination of higher premiums and greater cost sharing (relative to the other insurance plan types) as a way for the consumer to pay for the flexibility of provider choice and the relative inability for the insurer to control costs.
- Health maintenance organizations (HMOs) usually require that consumers see in-network providers to face the lowest cost-sharing levels for their OOP expenses for covered services. The consumer picks (or is assigned) a primary care provider when he or she joins the HMO.[25] Visits to specialists often require referrals (e.g., permission) from the consumer's primary care providers in order for the insurer to cover the visits. Network size varies across HMOs, as do the rules covering when the insured may go outside the network and receive coverage for medical services. The consumer's HMO insurance typically features some combination of lower premiums and lower levels of cost sharing (relative to the other health insurance plan types) to compensate for the restrictions on provider choice and to incorporate the insurer's ability to control costs.
- Preferred provider organizations (PPOs) offer intermediate amounts of consumer flexibility in provider choice to be eligible for full coverage. PPOs are associated with a given network. PPOs permit the insured to choose their own primary care providers and to visit specialists without a referral. Most PPOs will cover health care supplied out-of-network, but the cost sharing faced by the consumer will be higher than it would have been if the insured remained in-network. On average, PPOs typically feature intermediate premiums and levels of cost sharing (relative to the other health insurance plan types) because there are restrictions on provider choice in order to obtain the lowest levels of cost sharing and because the PPO insurer has weaker methods for cost control than does the HMO insurer.

Consumers may have mixed feelings about networks. Some may like the lower OOP expenses. However, some might discover that their chosen providers are not members of their particular network. In this case, a consumer might change providers, pay more OOP to use an out-ofnetwork provider, or change to a health insurance plan with a different network.

By Special Features

The "Cost Sharing" section above described select standard cost-sharing features of private health insurance. Some plan types, however, have specialized objectives. Two of these specialized plan types are consumer-directed health care (CDHC) and value-based insurance design (VBID). Both plan types have the potential to lower aggregate health care spending by reducing individual health spending. These plan types are designed to make consumers more aware of the costs of health care and lower consumers' OOP spending for especially valuable types of health care.

Consumer-Directed Health Care

CDHC encompasses any health care plan that provides monetary incentives for the consumers to become more active in their care by becoming well-informed and choosing practitioners and treatments that best suit their medical needs at the lowest possible costs. One prominent feature of CDHC is price transparency; the consumer is encouraged to find out what his or her OOP expenses will be for a potential health service. High-deductible health plans (HDHPs) are one type of insurance plan associated with CDHC. Consumers are thought to be especially sensitive to price in these plans because the consumers are spending 100% their own money until the high deductible is met.

Consumers with HDHPs sometimes have Health Savings Accounts (HSAs), which are tax-preferred savings accounts used to pay for unreimbursed qualified medical expenses such as health insurance deductibles, co-payments, and qualified services not covered by insurance.[26] HSAs are thought to encourage consumers to better save for their health care in retirement because any funds in the HSA accumulate from year to year.[27] Moreover, the combination of HDHPs and HSAs is thought to provide additional incentive for consumers to be more active in their care and to purchase the best possible medical services for the lowest possible cost because consumers may keep all the funds in the HSA and use them to pay for health care in retirement.

Value-Based Insurance Design

VBID reduces cost sharing for those health care goods and services that have strong evidence of relatively high clinical benefits.[28] VBID also may increase cost sharing for those health care goods and services with strong evidence of relatively low clinical benefits. In short, if a health care service provides substantial benefits for a particular group of consumers (or all consumers), the cost of the service for those consumers (or all consumers) should be lower.[29]

Consumers who might benefit from VBID insurance plans typically have predictable expenses for recurring health care with high clinical benefits. Consider a consumer with diabetes who takes long-lasting insulin. This type of insulin has a high clinical benefit, but it can be costly to the diabetic consumer. The principles of VBID suggest that health insurance plans have lower cost sharing for insulin than for other drugs. Therefore, the drug with the high clinical benefit becomes less expensive for diabetic consumers, who in turn become more likely to follow their prescribed dosing regimen because of the lower-than-usual cost.

By Actuarial Value

A consumer looking for a health insurance plan might want to compare plans by premiums and pick the plan with the lowest premium. Premiums, however, are not the only factor to consider when evaluating any particular plan; cost sharing, covered services, the composition of the network, and other factors also might matter. In addition, higher premiums may be associated with lower cost sharing and not with more comprehensive benefits. In this case, comparing premiums would not be an accurate comparison of plan benefits. Instead of premiums, actuarial values sometimes are used to compare health insurance policies because the plan's actuarial value is a better measure of plan comparability than is the plan's premium.

A health insurance plan's *actuarial value* is a summary measure of the plan's benefit generosity. It is expressed as a percentage of health care expenses for a standard population and a standard set of covered services estimated to be paid by the insurer. Two plans are actuarially equivalent if the estimated percentages of health care expenses paid by the plan for a given population are approximately equal. Nevertheless, two plans can be actuarially equivalent even though the details of their covered benefits and cost sharing differ.[30]

Which Health Insurance Plan Might Be Best for a Particular Consumer?

Some consumers might be able to choose from a large number of health insurance plans. A particular consumer's best plan depends on a number of factors, some of which have been discussed. This final section brings together several of the concepts introduced in the report.

Health Issues

Perhaps the most straightforward component of a consumer's selection of a health insurance plan concerns how many consumers the plan will cover. For example, is a self-only or family plan preferable? Another fairly straightforward consideration is the choice of health care providers. If the consumers to be covered already have chosen providers, or if they want to be able to choose providers at a later date (perhaps when they become sick), they need to investigate the network status of providers. The consumers can decide to restrict their choice to plans with networks in which their current providers participate, pay the higher OOP expenses associated with the use of out-of-network providers, or find new (in-network) providers.

It would seem like calculating which plans are affordable might be fairly straightforward for the consumer, because the consumer can find out the potential premiums and general levels of cost sharing before purchasing a plan. In addition, the consumer also has some idea of his or her (expected) income, assets, and other items that he or she might want or need to buy. However, affordability encompasses much more than premiums, cost sharing, and maximum OOP expenses. In particular, the consumer cannot know his or her OOP costs in advance. Despite the presence of clear cost-sharing rules, it is virtually impossible for the consumer to know how much and what type of health care he or she will need over the course of the year. Children may or may not get an ear infection, and an adult may or may not get colon cancer. A minor cough could turn out to be a cold, where no visit to a provider is needed, or it could be the flu, where a visit to a provider might be needed. As discussed in "The Challenges of Purchasing Health Care," a consumer can only approximate his or her health status and use of health services over the year, and therefore can only roughly approximate the affordability of various health insurance plans.

Employment Issues

In some cases, ESI offers the best value for health insurance policies.[31] But although there are advantages to obtaining ESI coverage, there are challenges as well. From the vantage point of the consumer, one of the biggest disadvantages is the general lack of portability. Because ESI coverage is tied to the job and not the person, any change in employment (such as going from full-time to part-time status or changing jobs) may alter the health plans, health care providers, or services to which the worker has access.[32] Indeed, the consumer may no longer be offered ESI after an employment change. In addition, the consumer's total compensation package may change when the employer offers ESI. Employers that offer health coverage may pay their employees lower wages because the employer uses the remainder of the employee's compensation package to pay for part of the employee's health insurance premiums. Workers who do not take up health insurance from their firms therefore may end up accepting lower wages for a set of benefits they do not use.

In short, determining which health insurance plan might be right for a particular consumer is far from simple. It involves, among other things, developing a sense of both what health care usage is likely to be over the term of the health insurance plan and the connections between health care and employment issues.

End Notes

[1] The precious metal designation corresponds to minimum actuarial value, which is discussed later in this report (see "By Actuarial Value"). In addition, more information is available in CRS Report R43854, Overview of Private Health Insurance Provisions in the Patient Protection and Affordable Care Act (ACA), by Annie L. Mach and Namrata K. Uberoi.

[2] The purchased plan may or may not cover additional members of the insured's family. Those who are at least aged 65 (and some disabled individuals) are eligible for the federal entitlement program Medicare.

[3] See CRS Report RL32237, Health Insurance: A Primer, by Bernadette Fernandez and Namrata K. Uberoi.

[4] This report deals only with private health insurance. Therefore, it does not cover public-sector programs such as Medicare, Medicaid, the State Children's Health Insurance Program (CHIP), and military health insurance. It also does not cover specialty insurance plans, such as those that cover vision, dental, or a specific disease (i.e., cancer).

[5] Insurers are also sometimes referred to as insurance firms and insurance carriers. A premium is the price of a health insurance plan.

[6] The term (length) of many health insurance policies is one year.

[7] Insurers also manage risk when providing health coverage to consumers to assure that their businesses are profitable. One type of risk management involves having a mix of consumers with different health statuses enrolled in each insurance product. The healthier consumers will be lower-cost enrollees, and the less-healthy consumers will be higher-cost enrollees. Were it permitted by federal and state law, an insurer would prefer to cover only the healthy.

[8] For more information, see CRS Report R41331, Individual Mandate Under ACA, by Annie L. Mach.

[9] Many employees receive two forms of compensation from their employers: wage (or salary) income and fringe benefits. Examples of fringe benefits include subsidized health insurance, subsidized day care, free coffee, and discounts on public transportation.

[10] Both the employer and the employee receive tax advantages from employer-sponsored insurance; for more information, see CRS Report RL32237, Health Insurance: A Primer, by Bernadette Fernandez and Namrata K. Uberoi.

[11] For a comprehensive guide to Medicare, see CRS Report R40425, Medicare Primer, coordinated by Patricia A. Davis and Scott R. Talaga.

[12] COBRA takes its name from Title X of the Consolidated Omnibus Budget Reconciliation Act of 1985 (P.L. 99-272). Under COBRA, employers are required to permit employees and family members to continue their group health insurance coverage at their own expense, but at group rates, if they lose coverage because of designated work- or family-related events.

[13] For more information, see CRS Report R43243, Health Insurance Exchanges: Health Insurance "Navigators" and In-Person Assistance, by Suzanne M. Kirchhoff.

[14] The exchanges described here are used by individuals. A second type of exchange, a Small Business Health Options Program (SHOP) exchange, is not covered in this report. For more information, see CRS Report R43771, Small Business Health Options Program (SHOP) Exchange.

[15] Any particular consumer may not have access to all of these coverage options.

[16] A health care provider is any individual who provides health care; doctors, nurse practitioners, licensed practical nurses, and physical therapists are examples of providers.

[17] This definition is found at https://www.healthcare.gov/glossary/medically-necessary, a government website managed by the U.S. Centers for Medicare & Medicaid Services.

[18] This coverage is mandated by the Women's Health and Cancer Rights Act, Title IX, Omnibus Consolidated and Emergency Supplemental Appropriations Act, 1998, P.L. 105-177.

[19] Hourly wages and annual salary are the conventional forms of compensation by the employer to the employee. The statement applies to all forms of compensation. This discussion ignores the effect of the employer's premium costs on the wages received by the employees; the last section of this report, "Employment Issues," provides more information.

[20] For more information, see CRS Report R41137, Health Insurance Premium Credits in the Patient Protection and Affordable Care Act (ACA) in 2014, by Bernadette Fernandez and the chart at https://www.healthcare.gov/qualifyingfor-lower-costs-chart.

[21] Grandfathered health insurance plans may impose cost-sharing requirements on preventive care. Grandfathered health insurance plans are plans in which a consumer was enrolled on March 23, 2010, and that meet a few additional criteria. For more information, see CRS Report R41166, Grandfathered Health Plans Under the Patient Protection and Affordable Care Act (ACA), by Bernadette Fernandez. A network is a group of providers that have agreed to provide health care under specified terms to those consumers who have signed up for a particular insurance plan. For more information on networks, see the section "By Networks and Flexibility in Choosing Providers."

[22] In this example, $150 is assumed to be at or under the maximum allowable charge of the insurer. The maximum allowable charge is the amount considered full payment by the insurer for this particular policy.

[23] Balance billing is the process of billing the patient for the difference between what the insurer reimburses and the provider charges. Consumers who use out-of-network providers may be subject to balance billing.

[24] Not all insurers use these terms when describing their plans.

[25] A primary care provider is responsible for the consumer's primary (as contrasted with specialized) care.

[26] The Internal Revenue Service determines whether a particular service is qualified. For more information, see Internal Revenue Service, Health Savings Accounts and Other Tax-Favored Health Plans, Publication 969, January 22, 2014, at http://www.irs.gov/pub/irs-pdf/p969.pdf.

[27] For more information on the incentives provided by high-deductible health plans and Health Savings Accounts, see archived CRS Report R41426, High-Deductible Health Plans and Health Savings Accounts: An Empirical Review, by Carol Rapaport.

[28] The information in this paragraph is from A. Mark Fendrick, Dean G. Smith, and Michael E. Chernew, "Applying Value-Based Insurance Design to Low-Value Health Services," Health Affairs, vol. 29, no. 11 (November 2010), at http://content.healthaffairs. org/content/29/11/2017.abstract.

[29] A value-based insurance design (VBID) plan may or may not be explicitly labeled as such. Any plan in which the level of cost sharing varies with the benefit of the medical service may be viewed as a VBID plan.

[30] Some health insurance policies are required to meet one of four levels of actuarial value. More specifically, plans offered in the individual and some small-group markets (both inside and outside exchanges) have this requirement. Each level is designated by a precious metal and corresponds to a specific actuarial value, as follows: bronze, 60% actuarial value; silver, 70% actuarial value; gold, 80% actuarial value; platinum, 90% actuarial value. As the plans move from bronze level to platinum level, all else equal, cost sharing generally decreases and premiums generally increase. In short, consumers usually must pay more for health insurance policies that cover more of their costs.

[31] Consumers who are relatively young and healthy might find options that are better for them through another source of health insurance.

[32] This scenario would occur when the providers associated with a worker's old network are not participants in any of the plans offered by the new employer.

In: Private-Sector Health Insurance
Editor: Stephen Maxwell Mathis

ISBN: 978-1-63483-772-9

Chapter 2

HEALTH INSURANCE: A PRIMER*

Bernadette Fernandez and Namrata K. Uberoi

SUMMARY

People obtain insurance to protect themselves against the possibility of financial loss in the future. Health insurance provides protection against the possibility of financial loss due to high health care expenses. Also, people do not know ahead of time exactly what their health care expenses will be, so paying for health insurance on a regular basis helps ease their out-of-pocket spending.

While health coverage continues to be mostly a private enterprise in this country, government plays an increasingly significant role. Government has initiated and responded to dynamics in medicine, the economy, and the workplace through legislation and public policies. One of the most recent efforts was enactment and ongoing implementation of the Patient Protection and Affordable Care Act (ACA; P.L. 111-148, as amended). ACA includes provisions to encourage the expansion of health insurance coverage, and establish new federal health insurance standards, among other reforms.

Americans obtain health insurance in different settings and through a variety of methods. In 2013, a majority (64.2%) of Americans obtained health insurance through the private sector, which includes both employer-sponsored and individual market coverage. Public programs

* This is an edited, reformatted and augmented version of a Congressional Research Service publication RL32237, prepared for Members and Committees of Congress dated January 8, 2015.

(Medicare, Medicaid/CHIP, or health services for military service members and veterans) provided coverage to 34.3% of Americans. Approximately 13.4% of Americans were uninsured for the entire year of 2013.

Health insurance benefits are delivered and financed under different systems. The factors that distinguish one delivery system from another are many, including how health care is financed, how much access to providers and services is controlled, and how much authority the enrollee has to design her/his health plan. To illustrate, managed care is characterized by predetermined restrictions on accessing services and providers, whereas individual decision-making regarding use of health benefits is a hallmark of consumer driven health care, such as health savings accounts. As economic conditions change, a specific delivery system may gain or lose the interest of affected parties.

INTRODUCTION

As health insurance coverage has evolved from an uncommon benefit to a routine one, government's role in subsidizing and regulating that coverage also has changed. While most insured Americans obtain health coverage through the private sector, public entities play an increasingly significant role.

The federal government's involvement in health coverage expanded dramatically over the past several decades:

- A long-standing rule issued by the Internal Revenue Service (IRS) in 1954 stated that an employer's contributions to employer-sponsored health insurance are not to be included in an employee's gross income for tax purposes (Internal Revenue Code, Section 106). This ruling helped spur the growth of employer-sponsored health benefits. The IRS also stated separately that employers could deduct such contributions as part of business expenses.
- Advances in medicine led to increased costs of treatment, which was especially problematic for certain groups of consumers who lacked health coverage. This led to government efforts to assist health care consumers in paying for medical services through the 1965 Medicare and Medicaid social insurance programs.[1]
- More and more employees began to work for more than one employer over their lifetimes. The federal government enacted the Health

Insurance Portability and Accountability Act of 1996 (HIPAA) to provide certain protections to workers that switched or lost jobs.
- In response to a persistent rate of uninsurance, the federal government in 2010 passed the Patient Protection and Affordable Care Act (ACA; P.L. 111-148, as amended), which instituted a large set of reforms to the private insurance market and expanded publicly funded coverage.

Given the frequent introduction of legislation aimed at modifying or building on the current health insurance system, understanding the potential impact of such proposals requires a working knowledge of how health insurance is provided, purchased, and regulated. This report provides background information about these topics.

WHAT IS HEALTH INSURANCE?

Definitions and Principles

People buy insurance to protect themselves against the possibility of financial loss in the future. Such losses may be due to a motor vehicle collision, natural disaster, or other circumstance. For individuals, financial losses may result from the substantial[2] use of health care services. Health insurance provides protection against the possibility of financial loss due to high health care expenses. Also, people do not know ahead of time exactly what their health care expenses will be, so paying for health insurance on a regular basis helps to smooth out their spending.

The concept underlying insurance is *risk* (i.e., the likelihood and magnitude of financial loss). In any type of insurance arrangement, all parties seek to minimize their own risk. In health insurance, consumers and insurers approach the management of insurance risk differently. From the consumer's point of view, a person (or family) buys health insurance to protect against financial losses resulting from the future use of medical care. From the insurer's point of view, it employs a variety of methods to manage the risk it takes on when providing health coverage to consumers, to assure that it operates a profitable business.[3] One method is to charge higher premiums for older consumers (to the extent allowed under federal law), because medical expenses tend to increase with age. While the methods employed by an insurer differ from those of a consumer, each has the same goal: to minimize risk in an uncertain future. It is this uncertainty of the future and risk of financial loss which form the context for insurance, and the strategies to make financial loss more predictable and manageable which drive insurance arrangements.

Risk Pools

A function of insurance is to spread risk across a group of people. This is achieved in health insurance when people contribute to a common pool (*risk pool*) an amount at least equal to the *expected* cost resulting from use of covered services by the group as a whole. In this way, the *actual* costs of health services used by a few people are spread over the entire group. This is the reason why insuring larger groups is considered less risky—the more individuals participating in a risk pool, the less likely that the serious medical experiences of one or a few persons will result in catastrophic financial loss for the entire pool.

An insurer calculates and charges a premium in order to finance the health coverage it provides. The premium reflects several components, including the expected cost of claims for health care use in a year, administrative expenses associated with running the plan, and a profit margin.[4] If the insurer accurately estimates future costs and sets appropriate premium levels for all enrollees, then that risk pool has reached equilibrium. This equilibrium is often achieved by healthy persons in the risk pool helping to subsidize the higher-than-average costs of less-healthy persons in the pool.

This redistributive effect is a primary feature of insurance, because it is generally understood that a minority of consumers is responsible for a majority of expenses. According to an analysis of national health care expenditure data, the top 5% of the population accounted for nearly half of all health expenditures in 2011 and 2012.[5] Because of this uneven distribution of expenses, in a risk pool it would be expected that costs attributed to those who incur the greatest expenses would be spread across the pool.

Risk Pool Composition and Adverse Selection

As noted above, one of the ways insurers attempt to make future costs more predictable is by spreading the risk of a few high-cost individuals across many people. But the number of people in a risk pool is not the only significant factor. Equally as important, if not more so, is the composition of the group.

A consumer's intention to obtain health coverage is based on a variety of factors, such as individual health status, estimated need for future medical care, and disposable income. Consumers with different health conditions, as well as varying degrees of comfort towards risk-taking, will differ on whether they consider health insurance necessary. However, with many companies offering their workers an employer subsidy for insurance plans, even those unlikely to incur significant medical expenses are incentivized to obtain coverage under this arrangement, if it is available to them. Because consumers are required by law (with certain individuals excepted) to either obtain insurance or face a penalty, their willingness to pay this penalty will also factor into their decision.[6]

Individuals who expect or plan for high use of health services tend to enroll in more generous (and consequently more expensive) health plans, a phenomenon known as *adverse selection*. An extreme example of adverse selection is when a disproportionate share of unhealthy people makes up a risk pool and the cost for each person in the pool rises. The higher costs may encourage the departure of healthier members and discourage the entrance of other healthy people, since healthier people may be able to find cheaper coverage elsewhere or decide that coverage is too costly and become uninsured (and pay a penalty). In either situation, it leaves an even less healthy group of people in the risk pool, which again causes the cost to rise for the remaining participants. If there is no change in this dynamic, the group may experience a self-reinforcing rise in costs as it suffers substantial adverse selection, leading to an increasingly expensive risk pool and possibly dissolution of the pool altogether.

Group and Nongroup Market

Health insurance can be provided to groups of people that are drawn together by an employer or other organization, such as a union. Such groups are generally formed for some purpose other than obtaining insurance, like employment. When insurance is provided to a group, it is referred to as *group coverage* or *group insurance*. In the group market, the entity that provides health benefits to the group (e.g., an employer) is referred to as the plan *sponsor*.

The group insurance market is divided into two segments, small group and large group, defined by the size of the employer or other organization purchasing a group insurance plan. Since some ACA reforms focus specifically on the small group insurance market, it is important to note the distinction in size between the small and large group markets. Before enactment of the ACA, the dividing line between small and large groups was typically 50 employees. In 2016, the dividing line will increase to 100 employees. Thus businesses with fewer than 100 employees will be defined as *small employers* and be eligible for small group coverage. Until the 100 employee large group definition takes effect in 2016, ACA allows states to choose whether to define *small employers* as those that employ 100 or fewer employees or those that employ 50 or fewer employees.[7]

Consumers who are not associated with a group can obtain health coverage by purchasing it directly from an insurer in the nongroup (*individual*) insurance market. The individual market enrolls many people who do not receive coverage from an employer—those who are self-employed, unemployed, or work part-time, and who are otherwise ineligible for public insurance programs like Medicare or Medicaid.

Fully Insured vs. Self-Insured Plans

A common distinction made between types of group health insurance products is whether they are fully insured or self-insured. A fully insured health plan is one in which the plan sponsor purchases health coverage from a state-licensed insurance carrier. The carrier assumes the risk of providing health benefits to the sponsor's enrolled members and the individuals/families directly purchasing individual insurance policies. In contrast, organizations that self-insure (or self-fund) do not purchase health coverage from insurers. Self-insured plans refer to health coverage that is provided directly by the organization seeking coverage for its members (e.g., a firm providing health benefits to its employees). Such organizations set aside funds and pay for health benefits directly. Under self-insurance, the organization bears the risk for covering medical expenses, and such benefit plans are not subject to state insurance regulations.8 Firms that self-insure may contract with third-party administrators (TPAs) to handle administrative duties such as member services, premium collection, and utilization review. TPAs do not underwrite insurance risk.

Self-Only vs. Family Coverage

Another common distinction made in health insurance refers to the scope of coverage provided under a health plan; that is, whether the coverage is for one person, a family, or other groupings. Under self-only coverage, the holder of the insurance policy is the only person insured. (Self-only coverage is also called individual coverage. Individual coverage in this sense should not be confused with health coverage from the individual insurance market—see discussion above.) Family coverage applies to the policyholder and his or her dependents. Other coverage arrangements may include self plus one, and self plus children.

Tax Exclusion for Employer-Sponsored Insurance

Health insurance coverage in the United States is delivered through a patchwork approach, which includes private and public sources, of providing and paying for health insurance and health care.

One of the key pieces of this approach encouraged the growth of employer-sponsored health coverage via the tax code.[9]

Section 106 of the Internal Revenue Code states that employer contributions to employer-sponsored health insurance are not included in workers' gross incomes for tax purposes. This tax preference encourages workers to sign up for (*take-up*) health coverage within the work setting. Moreover, employers' premium contributions are excluded from wages for the purpose of calculating employment taxes, which include Social Security and Medicare taxes, and unemployment taxes.[10] Exclusion of these contributions directly affects the amounts that employers and workers pay in taxes. In addition to the tax advantages, employer-sponsored health coverage allows both parties to benefit in other ways: employers use health insurance coverage as a means to recruit and retain workers, while workers have traditionally gained access to more plan choices at better rates than those seeking nongroup insurance (see discussion below). However, economic theory suggests that workers receive reduced wages to compensate for richer benefits.

The tax exclusion of health benefits is one of the primary reasons why health insurance coverage is provided mainly through the workplace in the United States. For example, approximately 53.9% of Americans had employer-sponsored insurance in 2013.[11] Furthermore, the tax exclusion of employer-sponsored insurance is the largest single tax expenditure by the federal government. The Congressional Budget Office estimated that the employer-sponsored health insurance exclusion from both income and payroll taxes would cost the government $248 billion in 2013.[12]

Health Insurance Premiums

A person enrolled in a private health insurance plan must pay a fee (*premium*), typically on a monthly basis, to maintain coverage under the plan. An insurer will then pay for a certain proportion of health care services and items at the time they are received (after the plan's deductible is met, if applicable), with the enrollee paying the rest of the cost out of pocket, an arrangement known as cost-sharing.

Premiums are used for three general purposes: payments for medical claims, administrative costs, and a profit margin. Claims payments make up the largest component of premiums, ranging from 85% to 88% of fully insured plans between 2006 and 2011.[13] The magnitude of claims payments is a function of both the *quantity* of health services (e.g., hospital visits) and items (e.g., prescription drugs) used and the *price* for each corresponding service and item (less any applicable enrollee cost-sharing), with rising prices, not quantity, generally being the main driver of total payments.[14] Administrative costs and a relatively modest profit margin—less than 5% in recent years[15]—make up the rest of premiums.

Premiums for U.S. insurance plans are difficult to summarize not only because plans can be arranged on behalf of a group by an organization such as an employer or purchased individually under a different set of regulations, but also because plans can cover a single person (self-only coverage), an entire family, or some combination in between. In addition, reliable premium information, especially for the nongroup market, can be difficult to find. Also, comparing premiums between groups is difficult considering the products (i.e. insurance) varies.

An annual source of employer health benefits data found that the average annual premium for self-only coverage was $6,025 in 2014. The average premium for a family of four was $16,834 that same year.[16] For self-only coverage, the cost of employer-sponsored health benefits was similar to the prior year. Compared to the previous year's average premiums, the cost for employer-sponsored health benefits for family coverage increased 3%. While this signals a reprieve from the double-digit increases that have occurred in the past, average premium growth rates still outpaced both wage growth and general inflation.[17]

Nongroup premiums have also risen in recent years. For instance, the individual market saw its national average rate of premium increase grow from 9.9% to 11.7% between 2008 and 2010.[18]

Administrative Expenses

Health insurance companies are complex organizations requiring specialized expertise and technology to develop, market, and operate a health plan. Administrative expenses include costs associated with contracting with providers, sales and marketing, enrollment and billing, customer service, utilization review, case management, and other functions. Given that administration is an essential component of an insurer's business, such expenses comprise an integral component of premiums.

Insurance companies report administrative costs in regulatory filings to applicable state entities. Such data indicate a relatively stable trend. From 2009 to 2013, general administrative expenses and claims adjustment expenses together took up between 11.7% and 12.1% of health insurers' net written premiums.[19]

Regulation of Health Insurance

Health insurance regulation addresses a wide variety of issues: the benefits that must be offered, the individuals to whom the insurance is made available, and the responsibilities insurers have to consumers, to name a few. One of the most enduring issues regarding health insurance regulation is whether it is the responsibility of individual states or the federal government.

Primary Responsibility of the States

The regulation of insurance traditionally has been a state responsibility, as clarified by the 1945 McCarran-Ferguson Act. Individual states have established standards and regulations overseeing the *business of insurance*, including requirements related to the finances, management, and business practices of an insurer. For example, all states have laws that require state-licensed insurance carriers to offer coverage for specified health services (*benefit mandates* or *mandated benefits*). Because fully-insured plans are subject to state-established requirements, those plans must offer those mandated benefits. On the other hand, self-insured plans are not subject to state insurance regulations so they are exempt from such requirements.

Key Federal Laws

Despite the states' role as the primary regulators of health insurance, overlapping federal requirements complicate regulation of the health insurance industry. Three federal laws in particular—the Employee Retirement Income Security Act of 1974 (ERISA; P.L. 93-406), the Health Insurance Portability and Accountability Act of 1996 (HIPAA; P.L. 104-191), and the Patient Protection and Affordable Care Act (ACA; P.L. 111-148, as amended)—have a significant impact on how private health insurance is provided.

ERISA outlines minimum federal standards for private-sector employer-sponsored benefits. (Public employee benefits and plans sponsored by churches are exempt from ERISA.) Passed in response to abuses in the private pension system, the Act was developed with a focus on pensions but the law applies to a long list of *welfare benefits*, including health benefits. ERISA requires that funds be handled prudently and in the best interest of beneficiaries, participants be informed of their rights, and there be adequate disclosure of a plan's financial activities. It preempts state laws that *relate to* employee benefit plans. (In other words, the federal law overrides state laws affecting private-sector employee benefits.) This portion of ERISA was designed to ensure that plans would be subject to the same benefit laws across all states, partly in consideration of firms that operate in multiple states. However, state laws still apply for issues which involve the *business of insurance*. The delineation of issues attributable to the phrases *relate to* and *business of insurance* is not clear, and has led to long-standing debates and active litigation over the scope of ERISA preemption.[20]

The core motivation behind the Health Insurance Portability and Accountability Act of 1996 (HIPAA) was to address the concern that insured persons had about losing their coverage if they switched jobs or changed health plans (*portability* of health coverage). The Act's health insurance provisions established federal requirements for private and public employer-sponsored health plans and insurers. These requirements included

- ensuring the availability and renewability of coverage for certain employees and other persons under specified circumstances,
- limiting the amount of time that coverage for preexisting medical conditions can be excluded, and
- prohibiting discrimination on the basis of health status-related factors.

The Act also includes tax provisions designed to encourage the expansion of health coverage through several mechanisms, such as authorizing tax-advantaged medical savings accounts, and a graduated increase of the portion of premiums self-employed persons may deduct from their federal income tax calculations.[21] Another set of HIPAA provisions addresses the electronic transmission of health information and the privacy of personally identifiable medical information (administrative simplification and privacy provisions, respectively).[22]

The 111th Congress passed comprehensive health reform legislation: the Patient Protection and Affordable Care Act (ACA; P.L. 111-148, as amended).[23] Enacted on March 23, 2010, and subsequently amended by a number of laws (including the Health Care and Education Affordability

Reconciliation Act of 2010; P.L. 111-152), ACA includes private insurance provisions that impose new requirements on individuals,[24] employers,[25] and health plans;[26] and provides financial assistance to certain individuals[27] and, in some cases, small employers.[28] These provisions include market reforms that impose certain requirements on private insurance plans and sponsors of insurance; establish insurance exchanges (*marketplaces*) where individuals and small businesses[29] can shop for and purchase health plans that meet or exceed federal standards; provide subsidies to certain individuals purchasing insurance from an exchange; establish an individual mandate for most individuals to purchase insurance or pay a penalty; and assess penalties on certain employers that do not provide insurance for their employees that meets preset standards of affordability and value.

SOURCES OF HEALTH INSURANCE

Americans obtain health insurance through a variety of methods and from different sources (see *Figure 1*). People may get it through the private sector or from a government source. Consumers may purchase health coverage on their own, as part of an employee group, or through a trade or professional association. Individuals can also have multiple sources of coverage in a year. That is, they may have multiple types of coverage at one time or even switch coverage types within a year.[30] This report discusses health insurance coverage in three categories: (1) insured through private sources, [31] (2) coverage under public programs,[32] or (3) uninsured.

Private Insurance

Private insurance, which includes both employer-sponsored (*group market*) and individual market (*nongroup*) coverage, accounts for the substantial majority of Americans with health insurance. In 2013, approximately 201 million individuals (64.2% of the U.S. population) received coverage through private insurance.[33]

The ACA introduced a number of significant reforms to the private insurance market, mostly directed to the individual and small group markets. Collectively, ACA's market reforms have substantially altered the landscape for private insurance.

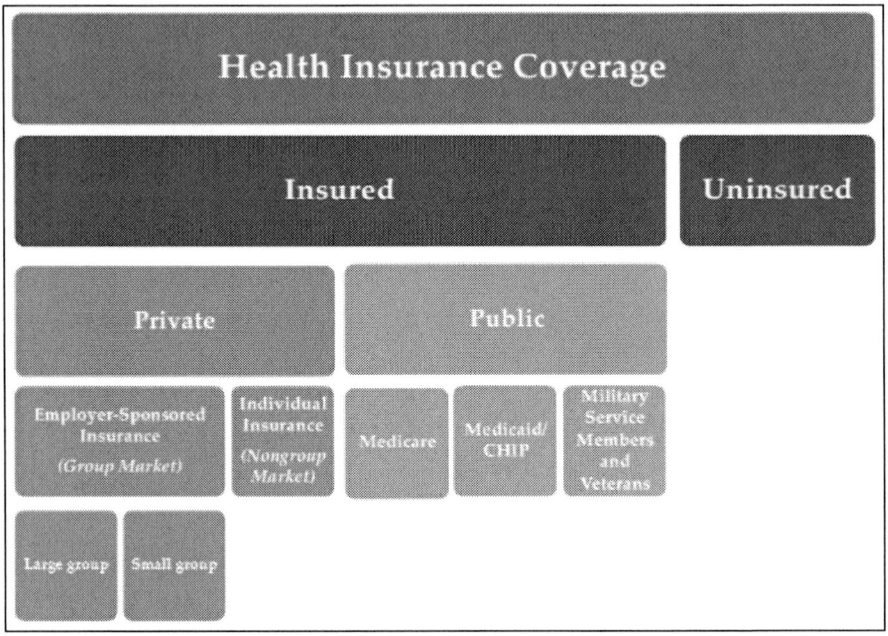

Source: Congressional Research Service (CRS) illustration of sources of health insurance coverage.

Notes: This figure is not drawn to scale; it is an illustration of the sources of health insurance and does not reflect their relative sizes.

Figure 1. Sources of Health Insurance.

Employer-Sponsored Insurance

Group health insurance is typically offered by employers, and most Americans obtain health coverage through the workplace. In 2013, approximately 169 million persons had employer-sponsored health insurance (ESI), which accounts for approximately 53.9% of the total U.S. population.[34]

Under ESI, risk pools may be comprised of active workers, dependents, and retirees. Insurers use a number of strategies to increase the likelihood that each risk pool includes a good proportion of healthy individuals. For instance, insurers may restrict employees' opportunities to take up health coverage or switch health plans by designating a specific time frame each year for such activities (*open enrollment period*). This strategy decreases the likelihood that people will *game* the system by taking up coverage only when they plan on using health services (e.g., for pregnancy and childbirth), and dropping coverage when they no longer plan to access care.[35] Employers also use strategies to encourage insurance take-up by healthy people. For example, employers typically make contributions that cover most of the health insurance premium. In 2014, employers paid more than 80% of the total premium amounts for self-only plans and more than 70% for family plans, on average.[36] This subsidy makes health coverage a more attractive benefit, even to those workers who do not plan to use medical services on a regular basis. By encouraging healthy workers to take-up health insurance, the employer subsidy helps to avoid adverse selection and contributes to the stability and diversity of the risk pool.

ESI has a number of strengths from the worker perspective. The employer premium contribution is exempt from individual income taxes, so workers are given a tax advantage by purchasing coverage through an employer compared with the individual insurance (*nongroup*) market. In addition, employer-sponsored coverage typically is heavily subsidized, so workers generally do not directly bear the full cost of insurance. Both the tax advantages and employer subsidy encourage the growth and continuity of ESI, historically providing an advantage over the individual market.[37]

For plan sponsors, health benefits are a common component of employee compensation used toward the recruitment and retention of workers. In addition, employers' premium contributions are excluded from wages for the purpose of calculating employment taxes, which directly affects the taxes owed by employers (and workers). Moreover, large employers that offer health coverage that meets certain standards will have complied with the ACA employer requirements, thus avoiding the employer tax for noncompliance.[38] Finally, certain small employers are eligible for small business tax credits if they contribute at least half of their employees' health insurance costs.[39]

While there are many advantages to obtaining ESI coverage, there are challenges as well. From the vantage point of the enrollee, one of the biggest disadvantages is the general lack of portability. Because ESI coverage is tied to the job and not the person, a change in employment (such as going from full-time to part-time status, or changing jobs) may alter the health care providers or services to which the worker has access, or disrupt health coverage altogether. Also, in firms that offer health coverage, there is a trade-off made between wages and benefits. For workers who do not take up health insurance from those firms, they end up accepting lower wages for a set of benefits they do not use. From the perspective of the plan sponsor, an underlying challenge is the lack of enrollee awareness of the true costs of health care. Because the sponsor usually contributes to the cost of the premium, enrollees do not bear the full cost of obtaining health coverage. Given this lack of awareness regarding total costs, sponsors' efforts to constrain their own health spending—by increasing the employee share of the premium or costsharing—are made even more difficult to justify or implement. Finally, from the perspective of the federal budget, the tax exclusion of employer-sponsored health insurance represents the largest source of foregone revenue.

Individual Health Insurance

The individual insurance (*nongroup*) market is referred to as a *residual* market, because it provides coverage to those who either cannot obtain health insurance through the workplace (i.e., employer-sponsored insurance) or do not qualify for public programs like Medicare, Medicaid, or the State Children's Health Insurance Program (CHIP). The residual nature of the individual insurance market is reflected in the demographic make-up of those who purchase coverage from it: many individuals with nongroup insurance are part-time workers, part-year workers, and self-employed persons—individuals who are unlikely to have access to employer coverage. In addition, some people use the individual insurance market as a temporary source of coverage, such as those in-between jobs or early retirees who are not yet eligible for Medicare.[40] The enrollee population of the market has also historically been small, with just 11% of the U.S. population covered by insurance purchased from the individual market in 2013.[41]

The insurance market reforms in the ACA specifically target the individual insurance market (as well as the small group market), in large part because the individual market lacked the advantages and protections compared with the large group market. Prior to ACA, individuals could be denied insurance altogether, charged a higher premium because of individual characteristics, and face benefit exclusions based on preexisting health conditions (if allowed under state law). State law varied greatly in terms of patient protections. ACA's market reforms and exchange provisions, which build on an existing but limited federal floor of insurance standards, affect the offer, issuance, generosity, and pricing of health plans, among other issues.[42] For example, ACA established a new tax credit that qualified individuals and families may use toward the purchase of insurance through exchanges.[43] Collectively, the market reforms and exchanges have transformed the plans and carrier practices in the individual insurance market, and standardized (to some degree) the patchwork of health regulation across the country.[44]

The ACA requires the establishment of a health insurance exchange in every state. ACA exchanges are marketplaces where individuals and small businesses can shop for and purchase private health insurance. The exchanges are intended to simplify the health insurance purchasing process and assist individuals in shopping for qualified health plans, applying for premium subsidies, enrolling in individual health plans, and even determining whether they qualify for Medicaid or other government programs. States can choose to run their own exchange, opt for a state-federal partnership, or have a federally facilitated exchange.[45]

Enrollment in the individual insurance market overall may increase due to ACA's market reforms, health insurance exchanges, and tax credits. The Congressional Budget Office and Joint Committee on Taxation project that by 2024, 25 million people under age 65 will be covered by nongroup insurance purchased from exchanges, representing a net increase in nongroup coverage of about 20 million.[46]

Public Programs

While most Americans with health insurance obtain it through the private sector, 107.6 million (34.3% of the U.S. population) people got health coverage through programs administered by the government in 2013.[47] Below are descriptions of selected public programs which provide health insurance coverage to eligible persons.

Medicare

In 2013, almost 49 million (15.6% of the U.S. population) individuals obtained coverage through Medicare.[48] The Medicare program was established in 1965, and is a federal program for persons age 65 and older and certain persons with disabilities. Medicare consists of four parts: Part A, Hospital Insurance; Part B, Supplementary Medical Insurance; Part C, Medicare Advantage; and Part D, the prescription drug benefit. The Medicare program provides coverage for a wide range of medical services, such as care provided in hospitals and skilled nursing facilities, hospice care, home health care, physician services, physical and occupational therapy, outpatient prescription drug benefits, and other services. Medicare has been so successful in covering the elderly that the problem of uninsurance usually is described in terms of the under-65 population.[49]

Medicaid and the State Children's Health Insurance Program

Medicaid covered approximately 54.1 million people (17.3% of the U.S. population) in 2013.[50] Medicaid is a joint federal and state program that finances the delivery of health care services to millions of low-income Americans. It is a means-tested program, and applicants must meet financial and other criteria in order to be eligible for services. Everyone who meets the eligibility criteria is entitled to Medicaid benefits available in their state of residence. Medicaid provides coverage for health care including primary and acute care as well as long-term services and supports to certain low-income adults, children, the elderly, and persons with disabilities. It is jointly funded by federal and state governments, and is administered by the states within federal guidelines. State Medicaid programs generally provide a comprehensive set of services, reflecting their diverse enrollee population. These programs must provide a set of federally-specified benefits for qualified individuals, such as hospital services (both inpatient and outpatient), physician services, nursing home care for individuals aged 21 and over, home health care, and certain services for children. States may also cover additional *optional services* and beneficiaries. Some states have used waiver authority under Medicaid to extend coverage to uninsured persons who do not meet the program's categorical and/or financial tests.[51] ACA includes provisions that significantly expand eligibility for Medicaid beginning in 2014, although individual states can elect not to participate in this expansion.[52]

The State Children's Health Insurance Program was established in 1997 to provide health coverage to uninsured low-income children who are ineligible for Medicaid. In designing their programs, states can choose among three options: expand Medicaid, create a separate CHIP program, or adopt a combination of both approaches. States that choose to expand Medicaid to CHIP eligibles must provide the full range of mandatory Medicaid benefits, as well as all optional services specified in their state Medicaid plans. States that establish CHIP programs that are separate from Medicaid choose one of three benefit options. All 50 states, the District of Columbia, and five territories have established some type of CHIP program. CHIP's eligibility rules target uninsured children under 19 years of age whose families' incomes are above Medicaid eligibility levels.[53]

Military Service Members and Veterans

In 2013, approximately 14.1 million persons (4.5% of the U.S. population) were covered by health care services for military service members and veterans.[54] Health care services for military service members and veterans are provided by the Department of Defense (DOD) through TRICARE or by the Department of Veterans Affairs (VA) through the VA system and the Civilian Health and Medical Program of the Department of Veterans Affairs (CHAMPVA).

The DOD administers health care services through the TRICARE program to eligible beneficiaries that include active duty uniformed personnel, eligible members of the Reserve Component, uniformed services retirees; as well as their dependents and survivors. TRICARE is administered on a regional basis and provides health services through military and nonmilitary hospitals, clinics, and providers.[55]

The Department of Veterans Affairs, through the Veterans Health Administration, operates the nation's largest integrated direct health care delivery system. The VA system is a veteran-specific national health care system in which the federal government owns the medical facilities and employs the health care providers. VA health care eligibility is based on veteran status, presence of service-connected disabilities or exposures, income, and/ or other factors.[56] Unlike TRICARE, VA health care covers a select group of dependents through CHAMPVA.[57]

The Uninsured

Despite the multiple sources of public and private health insurance coverage, millions of Americans are without health coverage. In 2013, approximately 42 million people (13.4% of the U.S. population) were without coverage.[58] For the vast majority of the uninsured, they lack coverage because they cannot *access* coverage (e.g., their employer does not offer health insurance as an employment benefit) or they cannot *afford* it.

Uninsurance is characterized as a problem of the under-65 population, given near-universal coverage of seniors through Medicare. One of the most striking characteristics of persons who lack coverage is that a significant proportion are in low-income families. For instance, among all uninsured persons under age 65, well over half were in poor or near-poor families in 2012.[59]

A defining characteristic of the nonelderly uninsured population is that most have ties to the paid labor force. In 2012, "just over 80 percent of the uninsured lived in families headed by workers."[60] While such findings may be counter-intuitive, there are multiple reasons why employed persons and their families may lack health coverage. For example, a worker may be offered health insurance by his/her employer, but declines it because he/she thinks it is too expensive. An employee may work for a small firm which is less likely than a large firm to offer health insurance as a benefit. Finally, a healthy worker may be willing to take on the risk of being uninsured and choose not to purchase insurance at all. So, despite the dominance of employer-sponsored health insurance, the dynamics of employment status, health conditions, and financial resources intersect to historically impede coverage of all workers and their families.

Consequences of Uninsurance

While health insurance coverage is not necessary to obtain health care, it is a useful mechanism for accessing services in an environment of increasingly expensive health care. As health care costs continue to rise, more people need greater assistance with covering medical expenses. Health insurance provides some measure of protection for consumers, especially for those who have limited means or greater-than-average need for medical care.

Health insurance is considered important also because of the well-documented, far-reaching consequences of uninsurance. For instance, uninsured persons are more likely to forgo needed health care than people with health coverage.[61] This includes forgoing services for preventable or chronic conditions, which often leads to worse health outcomes. Uninsured persons also are less likely to have a *usual source of care*, that is, a person or place identified as the source to which the consumer *usually* goes for health services or medical advice (not including emergency rooms). Having a usual source is important because people who establish ongoing relationships with health care providers or facilities are more likely to access preventive health services and have regular visits with a physician, compared with individuals without a usual source.[62]

The ACA now requires most individuals to maintain health insurance coverage for themselves and their dependents, or otherwise pay a penalty. Some individuals are exempt[63] from the individual mandate and the penalty. Individuals who do not maintain minimum essential coverage and are not exempt from the mandate will have to pay a penalty for each month of noncompliance. In 2014, the annual penalty was the greater of $95 or 1% of applicable income. In 2015, the annual penalty is the greater of $325 or 2% of applicable income.[64]

Expanding coverage is one of the primary objectives of the ACA. The Congressional Budget Office and the Joint Committee on Taxation estimated that ACA will increase the number of nonelderly Americans with health insurance by about 26 million by 2024 relative to the projected trend without ACA. The share of nonelderly U.S. residents with insurance coverage in 2024 is estimated to be around 89%, compared with a projected share of around 80% in the absence of the law. However, approximately 31 million nonelderly U.S. residents are estimated to remain uninsured, including individuals who choose not to purchase health insurance and are subject to the penalty for non-compliance to the ACA's individual mandate, individuals who are exempt from the individual mandate, and undocumented individuals.[65]

CONCLUSION

Health insurance in the United States is a patchwork comprised of a combination of private and government sources. In 2013, a majority (64.2%) of Americans obtained health insurance through the private sector, which includes both employer-sponsored and nongroup coverage. Public programs (Medicare, Medicaid/CHIP, or health care services for military service members and veterans) provided coverage to 34.3% of Americans. Approximately 13.4% of Americans were uninsured for the entire year of 2013.[66,67]

Within each of the sources, health insurance differs by the market structure itself—group versus nongroup, fully insured versus self-insured; self-only versus family coverage, etc. Overlaying this patchwork are also regulations from both the federal and state level. In addition, the ACA instituted a large set of reforms to the private insurance market and expanded publicly funded coverage. Health care is also delivered and financed through different arrangements (e.g., indemnity insurance, managed care, and consumer-driven health care), which are further discussed in the *Appendix*. The popularity of some of these mechanisms has also changed over time.

APPENDIX. HOW IS PRIVATE HEALTH COVERAGE PROVIDED?

Given the complexity of the health care system overall, it is no surprise that health coverage is delivered and financed through different arrangements. Those arrangements vary due to numerous factors such as how health care is financed, how much access to providers and services is controlled, and how much flexibility the enrollees have to use the services covered under her/his health plan. While delivery systems may share certain characteristics, general distinctions can be made based on payment, access, and other critical variables.

Indemnity Insurance

Under indemnity insurance, the insured person decides when and from whom to seek health services. If the services the enrollee receives are covered under his/her insurance, the enrollee or the enrollee's provider files a claim with the insurer. Thus, insurers make payments *retrospectively* (i.e., after the health services have been rendered), up to the maximum amounts specified for each covered service. In this model of health care delivery, the financing of health services and the obtaining of those services are kept separate.

This bifurcated arrangement was unquestioned for a time. But as medical costs began to rise, sometimes faster than other sectors of the national economy, many observers criticized this delivery model as contributing to increasing expenditures. Because providers were compensated on a fee-for-service basis, some argued that providers were not given incentives to provide efficient health care. In fact, some critics accused health care practitioners and institutions of providing an over-abundance of health care in order to generate greater revenue.[68] By the early 1970s, legislators, analysts, and others expressed considerable interest in alternative models, such as managed care models, with cost control as a key feature.

Managed Care

While managed care means different things to different people, several key characteristics set it apart from traditional (indemnity) insurance. One of the main differences is that the service delivery and financing functions are integrated under managed care. Managed care organizations (MCOs) employ various techniques to control costs and manage health service use *prospectively*. Among those techniques are restricting enrollee access to certain providers (*in-network* providers); requiring primary-care-physician approval for access to specialty care (*gatekeeping*); coordinating care for persons with certain conditions (*disease management* or *case management*); and requiring prior authorization for routine hospital inpatient care (*pre-*

certification). MCOs may offer different types of health plans that vary in the degree to which cost and medical decision-making is controlled. As a consequence, enrollee costs also vary. Generally, the more tightly managed a plan is, the lower the premium. Other distinguishing features of the managed care approach include an emphasis on preventive health care and implementation of quality assurance processes.

Managed care was touted as the antidote to rapidly rising health care costs. Starting with the passage of federal legislation in the 1970s which supported the growth of managed care (specifically in the form of health maintenance organizations (HMOs)), the number of MCOs grew quickly. Increased market competition among these organizations led to decreases in premiums, in order to gain market share. With high medical inflation in the 1980s and early 1990s, enrollees flocked to these less-costly managed care plans. By the mid-1990s, more insured workers were enrolled in HMOs than any other health plan type—contributing to the substantial displacement of traditional indemnity insurance[69]—and health insurance premiums had stabilized.[70]

But in the latter half of the 1990s, a *backlash* against managed care started to grow.[71] Some enrollees had grown weary of provider and service restrictions. Many MCOs that had increased market share through artificially low premiums began to raise them in order to increase revenue.[72] Consumers and others accused the managed care industry of caring more about controlling costs than providing health care.[73] Some providers resented the role managed care played in medical decision-making. Many enrollees began to leave HMOs. The industry responded by developing insurance products that were less-tightly managed, but more costly. Some traditional HMOs widened their provider networks and eliminated the gatekeeping function, while employers began to offer plan types that were less tightly managed, such as preferred provider organizations (PPOs).[74] In fact, by the end of the 1990s, more people with work-based health coverage were enrolled in PPOs than in HMOs.[75]

As the influence of managed care waned and health care costs began to rise at an increasing pace during the late 1990s, consumers began to feel the impact. For example, in the employment setting, employers absorbed the extra costs at first in order to recruit and retain workers during the booming economy of the mid to late 1990s.[76] But as the economy soured, employers began to pass these expenses along to enrollees by increasing employees' contributions to their own coverage.[77]

Consumer-Driven Health Care

By the end of the 1990s, large increases in health costs again became commonplace. With the belief by some observers that the age of managed care was over, they began to search for alternatives. Consumer-driven (or consumer-directed) health care has been offered as one such option.

Consumer-driven health care refers to a broad spectrum of coverage arrangements that give incentives to consumers to control their use of health services and/or ration their own health benefits. While consumer-driven health care can take on many forms, the premise common to all of these approaches is that by making enrollees more responsible for the cost of their own health care, it creates incentives for people to use services prudently. The expectation is that greater cost-consciousness on the part of consumers will result in lower overall health costs. In essence, the service and cost control functions administered by MCOs and providers under managed care shifts in part to enrollees under the consumer-driven health care model.

One example that is at the heart of discussions about consumer-driven care is the health savings account (HSA). An HSA, in and of itself, is not a health insurance plan. Instead, it is an investment account in which contributions earn interest tax free. Consumers, their employers, or both may make contributions to HSAs. Consumers withdraw funds on a tax-free basis to cover medical expenses not covered by health insurance. Unused contributions roll over to the next year. HSAs are paired with high-deductible health plans. If the HSA funds are exhausted and the deductible level has not been reached, the consumer is responsible for covering that gap. Once the consumer's spending reaches the deductible level, then coverage from the health plan takes effect. HSAs were authorized in November 2003 under the Medicare Prescription Drug, Improvement, and Modernization Act of 2003 (P.L. 108-173).[78]

Proponents of consumer-directed health care assert the merit in having people take increased responsibility for their own health care use and expenses. They predict that this approach will lead to better-informed consumers, more appropriate use of health services, and lower overall spending on health care. Opponents express concern that this approach does not recognize the possible range of health conditions in an enrolled population; and imposes a greater burden on individuals with moderate to severe health conditions. Also, opponents point out that the tax advantages of such insurance arrangements benefit the wealthy to a greater extent than those less well off.

Recent Enrollment Trends

From the mid-1990s to 2014, HMOs continued to become proportionally less popular among covered workers, declining to a 13% share of the employer-sponsored insurance market in 2014 after reaching a 31% share in 1996. For more than a decade, PPOs have made up the majority (58% share in 2014) of employer-sponsored plans—contributing to the displacement of conventional indemnity coverage, which has by now all but disappeared from the private market. PPO plans, which combine moderate provider network restrictions with increased patient freedom relative to HMOs, remain the dominant form of worker coverage today. High-deductible coverage paired with HSAs and other savings account arrangements have also made inroads in the market, making up about a fifth of employer-sponsored enrollment by 2014.[79]

The individual insurance market has seen a similar distribution of plan types. Surveys taken of health insurers show that for the individual market, just as for the group market, PPOs are the most popular option; in fact, they are overwhelmingly popular, accounting for more than 80% of self-only plans and more than 70% of family plans in 2009. In contrast, HMOs are relatively unpopular, with HMO plans declining from about 6% of self-only plans in 2004 to about 2% in 2009.[80]

End Notes

[1] Publicly funded health programs generally either provide funding for direct medical services or assist consumers in paying for health care. The latter are included in a broad category of programs based on social insurance principles. Social insurance refers to publicly funded insurance programs that are statutorily mandated for certain groups of people, such as low-income individuals.

[2] Either in terms of multiple services due to a chronic condition or a single use due to an emergency condition.

[3] While nonprofit organizations also provide health insurance in this country, such organizations nonetheless are interested in containing expenses, even if they do not have a profit motive.

[4] The premium calculation is further adjusted to reflect a variety of factors collectively known as the underwriting cycle.

[5] S. Cohen, "The Concentration and Persistence in the Level of Health Expenditures over Time: Estimates for the U.S. Population, 2011-2012," September 2014, http://meps.ahrq.gov/mepsweb/data_files/publications/st449/stat449.pdf.

[6] For additional information on the individual mandate under ACA, see CRS Report R41331, Individual Mandate Under ACA.

[7] For additional information on the ACA's insurance standards, see CRS Report R42069, Private Health Insurance Market Reforms in the Affordable Care Act (ACA).

[8] For further discussion, see "Regulation of Health Insurance."

[9] The federal tax code contains many health-related provisions that provide tax advantages to certain individuals, employers and workers, for both the purchase of health coverage and unreimbursed medical expenses. For additional information about health-related tax benefits, see Joint Committee on Taxation, "Tax Expenditures for Health Care," July 30, 2008, available at https://www.jct.gov/publications.html?func=select&id=5.

[10] 26 U.S.C. §§ 3121(a)(2), 3231(e)(1), and 3306(b)(2).

[11] U.S. Census Bureau, Current Population Survey, "Health Insurance Coverage in the United States: 2013," September 2014, available at http://www.census.gov/content/dam/Census/library/publications/2014/demo/p60-250.pdf.

[12] Congressional Budget Office, "Options for Reducing the Deficit: 2014 to 2023," November 2013, available at http://cbo.gov/sites/default/files/cbofiles/attachments/44715-OptionsForReducingDeficit-3.pdf.

[13] Debra A. Donahue, "Medical Expense Trend Up in 2011," Mark Farrah Associates, February 12, 2013, available at http://www.markfarrah.com/healthcare-business-strategy/Medical-Expense-Trend-Up-in-2011.aspx.

[14] Health Care Cost Institute, "2013 Health Care Cost and Utilization Report," October 2014, http://www.healthcostinstitute.org/files/2013%20HCCUR%2012-17-14.pdf.

[15] Debra A. Donahue, "Medical Expense Trend Up in 2011," Mark Farrah Associates, February 12, 2013, available at http://www.markfarrah.com/healthcare-business-strategy/Medical-Expense-Trend-Up-in-2011.aspx.

[16] These averages include both the employer and employee shares of the total premium. The Kaiser Family Foundation and Health Research and Educational Trust, 2014 Employer Health Benefits Survey, available online at http://files.kff.org/attachment/2014-employer-health-benefits-survey-full-report.

[17] Ibid.

[18] Jonathan Gruber, "Growth and Variability in Health Plan Premiums in the Individual Insurance Market Before the Affordable Care Act." The Commonwealth Fund. June 2014. Available at http://www.commonwealthfund.org/~/media/files/publications/issue-brief/2014/jun/1750_gruber_growth_variability_hlt_plan_premiums_ib_v2.pdf.

[19] National Association of Insurance Commissioners, "2013 Health Insurance Industry Analysis Report," available at http://www.naic.org/documents/topic_insurance_ industry_ snapshots_2013_industry_analysis_report.pdf.

[20] For additional information about ERISA, see the Department of Labor's overview document for a summary and relevant links, http://www.dol.gov/dol/topic/health-plans/erisa.htm#doltopics.

[21] For additional information about this tax deduction, see Internal Revenue Service, IRS Tax Tip 2013-43, March 28, 2013, available at http://www.irs.gov/uac/Newsroom/Dont-Miss-the-Health-Insurance-Deduction-if-Youre-SelfEmployed.

[22] For FAQs regarding HIPAA's health insurance provisions, see http://www.dol.gov/ebsa/faqs/faq_consumer_hipaa.html.

[23] For additional information on ACA provisions that affect private insurance, see CRS Report R43048, Overview of Private Health Insurance Provisions in the Patient Protection and Affordable Care Act (ACA).

[24] For additional information, see CRS Report R41331, Individual Mandate Under ACA.

[25] For additional information, see CRS Report R41159, Potential Employer Penalties Under the Patient Protection and Affordable Care Act (ACA).

[26] For additional information, see CRS Report R42069, Private Health Insurance Market Reforms in the Affordable Care Act (ACA).

[27] For additional information, see CRS Report R41137, Health Insurance Premium Credits in the Patient Protection and Affordable Care Act (ACA).

[28] For additional information, see CRS Report R41158, Summary of the Small Business Health Insurance Tax Credit Under ACA.

[29] For additional information, see CRS Report R43771, Small Business Health Options Program (SHOP) Exchange.

[30] Individuals may report more than one source of coverage, and individuals may report both private insurance and insurance through public programs; therefore, percentages presented in this report total to more than 100.

[31] Private health insurance includes employer-sponsored insurance and individual market insurance.

[32] Public programs include Medicare, Medicaid and other means-tested public programs (e.g., the State Children's Health Insurance Program, CHIP), and health care services for military service members and veterans (e.g., TRICARE).

[33] U.S. Census Bureau, Current Population Survey, "Health Insurance Coverage in the United States: 2013," September 2014, available at http://www.census.gov/content/dam/Census/library/publications/2014/demo/p60-250.pdf.

[34] U.S. Census Bureau, Current Population Survey, op. cit.

[35] Under the ACA's individual mandate, those who decline coverage from an employer and do not take up any other coverage may be subject to a penalty. For additional information, see CRS Report R41331, Individual Mandate Under ACA.

[36] The Kaiser Family Foundation and Health Research and Educational Trust, 2014 Employer Health Benefits Survey, available online at http://files.kff.org/attachment/2014-employer-health-benefits-survey-full-report.

[37] ACA's reforms to the nongroup market and establishment of exchanges and tax credits are policy levers to make the nongroup market behave more like the large group market. See the section titled "Individual Health Insurance" in this report for additional information about these issues.

[38] For additional information about this issue, see CRS Report R41159, Potential Employer Penalties Under the Patient Protection and Affordable Care Act (ACA).

[39] For additional information about small business tax credits under ACA, see CRS Report R41158, Summary of the Small Business Health Insurance Tax Credit Under ACA.

[40] Kaiser Family Foundation, "Survey of People Who Purchase Their Own Insurance," June 2010, http://kaiserfamilyfoundation.files.wordpress.com/2013/01/8077-r.pdf.

[41] U.S. Census Bureau, Current Population Survey, op. cit.

[42] For a discussion of these and other insurance market reforms in the ACA, see CRS Report R42069, Private Health Insurance Market Reforms in the Affordable Care Act (ACA).

[43] See CRS Report R41137, Health Insurance Premium Credits in the Patient Protection and Affordable Care Act (ACA).

[44] Private health insurance is primarily regulated at the state-level. The ACA establishes uniform requirements and additional options for all states.

[45] Currently, 14 states and DC have their own state-based exchanges and the remaining 36 states are participating in the Federally-facilitated Marketplace or have State Partnership Marketplaces or supported State-based Marketplaces.

[46] The 2024 projected exchange enrollment of 25 million is partially offset by a decrease of 5 million in nongroup coverage outside of the exchanges. A very small portion of this projected decrease includes other forms of coverage. Congressional Budget Office, "Updated Estimates of the Effects of the Insurance Coverage Provisions of the Affordable Care Act, April 2014," available at http://cbo.gov/sites/default/files/cbofiles/ attachments/ 45231- ACA_Estimates.pdf.

[47] U.S. Census Bureau, Current Population Survey, op. cit.

[48] U.S. Census Bureau, Current Population Survey, op. cit.

[49] For additional information about Medicare, see CRS Report R40425, Medicare Primer.

[50] U.S. Census Bureau, Current Population Survey, op. cit.

[51] For additional information about Medicaid, see CRS Report R43357, Medicaid: An Overview.

[52] For additional information about the expansion of Medicaid under ACA, see CRS Report R43564, The ACA Medicaid Expansion.

[53] For additional information about CHIP, see CRS Report R40444, State Children's Health Insurance Program (CHIP): A Brief Overview.

[54] U.S. Census Bureau, Current Population Survey, op. cit.

[55] For additional information on TRICARE and the military health system, see CRS Report RL33537, Military Medical Care: Questions and Answers.

[56] Other factors include status as a former prisoner of war or receipt of a Purple Heart.

[57] For additional information on health care for veterans and CHAMPVA, see CRS Report R42747, Health Care for Veterans: Answers to Frequently Asked Questions.

[58] U.S. Census Bureau, Current Population Survey, op. cit.

[59] Persons with income at or below 250% of the federal poverty level accounted for about 75% of all nonelderly uninsured individuals in 2012. Kaiser Family Foundation, "The Uninsured: A Primer – Key Facts about Health Insurance on the Eve of Coverage Expansions," October 2013, http://kff.org/uninsured/report/the-uninsured-a-primerkey-facts-about-health-insurance-on-the-eve-of-coverage-expansions/.

[60] Ibid., p. 17.

[61] Kaiser Commission on Medicaid and the Uninsured, "The Uninsured and the Difference Health Insurance Makes," Oct. 2011, http://www.kff.org/uninsured/upload/1420-13.pdf.

[62] Agency for Healthcare Research and Quality, "National Healthcare Disparities Report, 2013," May 2014, http://www.ahrq.gov/research/findings/nhqrdr/nhdr13/2013nhdr.pdf.

[63] There are many different types of exemptions, such as hardship, affordability, qualifying religious reasons, membership in health care sharing ministry, not lawfully present in the U.S., etc.

[64] For additional information on the individual mandate, see CRS Report R41331, Individual Mandate Under ACA.

[65] Congressional Budget Office, "Updated Estimates of the Effects of the Insurance Coverage Provisions of the Affordable Care Act, April 2014." Available at http://cbo.gov/sites/ default/files/cbofiles/attachments/45231- ACA_Estimates.pdf.

[66] U.S. Census Bureau, Current Population Survey, "Health Insurance Coverage in the United States: 2013," September 2014, available at http://www.census.gov/content/dam/ Census/library/publications/2014/demo/p60-250.pdf.

[67] Individuals may report more than one source of coverage, and individuals may report both private insurance and insurance through public programs; therefore percentages total to more than 100.

[68] "The Role of Prepaid Group Practice in Relieving the Medical Care Crisis," Harvard Law Review, vol. 84, no. 4 (Feb. 1971), pp. 887-1001. Available at http://www. jstor. org/stable/1339782.

[69] The Kaiser Family Foundation and Health Research and Educational Trust, 2014 Employer Health Benefits Survey, available online at http://files.kff.org/attachment/2014-employer-health-benefits-survey-full-report.

[70] Jon Gabel, et al., "Job-Based Health Benefits in 2002: Some Important Trends," Health Affairs, vol. 21, no. 5, pp. 143-151.

[71] Richard Kronick, "Waiting for Godot: Wishes and Worries in Managed Care," Journal of Health Politics, Policy and Law, vol. 24, no. 5, pp. 1099-1106.

[72] Jon Gabel et al., "Job-Based Health Insurance in 2001: Inflation Hits Double Digits, Managed Care Retreats," Health Affairs, vol. 20, no. 5, pp. 180-186.

[73] Firshein J, Sandy LG. The changing approach to managed care. In: Isaacs SL, Knickman JR, eds. To Improve Health and Health Care 2001: The Robert Wood Johnson Anthology. San Francisco: Jossey-Bass; 2001:77-100.

[74] PPOs allow plan participants and beneficiaries to use any health care provider, but offer lower cost-sharing when individuals use in-network providers, with whom the insurer has negotiated rates.

[75] The Kaiser Family Foundation and Health Research and Educational Trust, 2014 Employer Health Benefits Survey, available online at http://files.kff.org/attachment/2014-employer-health-benefits-survey-full-report.

[76] Jon B. Christianson and Sally Trude, "Managing Costs, Managing Benefits: Employer Decisions in Local Health Care Markets," Health Services Research, pt. II, vol. 38, no. 1, pp. 357-373.

[77] Jon Gabel, et al., "Job-Based Health Benefits in 2002: Some Important Trends," Health Affairs, vol. 21, no. 5, pp. 143-151.

[78] For additional information about HSAs, see CRS Report RS22877, Health Savings Accounts and High-Deductible Health Plans: A Data Primer.

[79] The Kaiser Family Foundation and Health Research and Educational Trust, 2014 Employer Health Benefits Survey, available online at http://files.kff.org/attachment/2014-employer-health-benefits-survey-full-report.

[80] America's Health Insurance Plans Center for Policy and Research, Individual Health Insurance 2009: A Comprehensive Survey of Premiums, Availability, and Benefits. Oct. 2009. Available at http://www.ahip.org/ Individual-Health-Insurance-Survey-2009/. America's Health Insurance Plans Center for Policy and Research. Individual Health Insurance: A Comprehensive Survey of Affordability, Access, and Benefits. Aug. 2005. Available at http://heartland.org/sites/all/modules/custom/heartland_migration/ files/pdfs/ 17693.pdf. Plan type information was not grouped in the same way across survey years, potentially leading to slight discrepancies between surveys. However, the broader picture illustrated by the numbers is correct.

In: Private-Sector Health Insurance
Editor: Stephen Maxwell Mathis
ISBN: 978-1-63483-772-9

Chapter 3

OVERVIEW OF PRIVATE HEALTH INSURANCE PROVISIONS IN THE PATIENT PROTECTION AND AFFORDABLE CARE ACT (ACA)*

Annie L. Mach and Namrata K. Uberoi

SUMMARY

Private health insurance (PHI) is the predominate form of health insurance coverage in the United States, covering about two-thirds of Americans in 2013. The Patient Protection and Affordable Care Act (ACA; P.L. 111-148, as amended) builds on existing sources of private health insurance coverage—the nongroup (*individual*), small group, and large group markets. The ACA private health insurance provisions follow a federalist model in which they establish federal minimum requirements and give states the authority to enforce and expand those federal standards.

The ACA includes provisions that restructure the private health insurance market by

* This is an edited, reformatted and augmented version of a Congressional Research Service publication R43854, prepared for Members and Committees of Congress, dated January 8, 2015.

- implementing market reforms that impose requirements on insurers and sponsors of health insurance (e.g., employers);
- instituting a core set of benefits and services (i.e., the essential health benefits);
- establishing an individual mandate that requires most individuals to either maintain health insurance coverage or pay a penalty;
- creating exchanges (*marketplaces*) in which individuals and small businesses can shop for and purchase health plans that meet or exceed federal standards;
- providing financial assistance to qualified individuals who purchase health plans through an exchange; and
- assessing penalties on certain employers that either do not provide health insurance or provide health insurance that is *unaffordable* or does not provide *minimum value*.

BACKGROUND

Americans obtain health insurance coverage in different settings and through a variety of methods. Although many receive coverage through publicly funded programs (e.g., Medicare and Medicaid), private health insurance is the predominate form of health coverage in the United States. The private market is often described as having three segments: nongroup (*individual*), small group, and large group.[1] In 2013, about 64.2% of the population had private health insurance.[2] Most individuals and families obtain private insurance through small or large group coverage, such as employer-sponsored insurance; some individuals and families may purchase private insurance on their own in the nongroup market.

The Patient Protection and Affordable Care Act (ACA; P.L. 111-148, as amended) includes several provisions that affect the private health insurance market. These provisions create federal rules and incentives for entities and individuals in the market that build on and modify the existing market structure. Collectively, the provisions reflect the ACA's general goal of increasing access to health insurance coverage.

The ACA also includes an individual mandate, which requires most individuals to maintain health insurance coverage or pay a penalty for noncompliance. Many have argued that unless healthy individuals are encouraged to participate in the private market, insurance pools will primarily consist of individuals who are high users of health care services, potentially creating financially unstable situations for insurers and enrollees.[3] As of

January 1, 2014, most individuals are required to maintain health insurance coverage or otherwise pay a penalty.

Under the ACA, nearly all individuals can obtain private coverage regardless of preexisting conditions or health status and insurers have limited ability to vary premiums based on an applicant's health status and other characteristics. To help accommodate individuals who have access to private health insurance as a result of these (and other) provisions, individuals and small businesses can shop for and purchase private coverage in health insurance exchanges (*marketplaces*). Additionally, some individuals can receive financial assistance toward coverage obtained in an exchange.

The ACA provides financial incentives for employers to consider when determining whether to offer employer-based health insurance to employees. Some small employers are eligible to receive tax credits for their contributions toward their employees' health insurance premiums. Certain large employers are subject to a *shared responsibility* provision. This provision does not explicitly mandate that a large employer offer employees health insurance; instead, it has the potential to impose penalties on large employers that do not provide affordable and adequate coverage to their employees. The shared responsibility provision was slated to take effect in 2014, but its implementation was delayed until 2015.

This report describes various ACA provisions that affect the private insurance market.

PRIVATE HEALTH INSURANCE MARKET REFORMS

Exemptions from ACA Market Reforms

Grandfathered Status

Health insurance plans that were in existence (either in the group or nongroup market) and in which at least one person was enrolled on the date of the ACA's enactment (March 23, 2010) are considered grandfathered and have a unique status under the ACA. As long as a plan maintains its grandfathered status, the plan has to comply with some but not all ACA provisions. Plans may lose their status if they apply certain changes to benefits, cost-sharing, employer contributions, and access to coverage.

Transitional Policy

On March 5, 2014, the Centers for Medicare and Medicaid Services (CMS) extended a transitional policy that was first described in guidance issued by CMS in November 2013. Under the transitional policy, health insurance issuers offering non-grandfathered coverage in the nongroup and small group markets may choose to continue coverage that would otherwise be canceled. Pursuant to the policy, state insurance commissioners may choose whether to enforce compliance with specified ACA market reforms. Presumably, if state insurance commissioners choose not to enforce compliance, then issuers may renew coverage for enrollees who would otherwise receive cancellation notices. Pursuant to the extended policy, coverage renewed for a plan year beginning before or on October 1, 2016, does not have to comply with certain ACA market reforms, provided the coverage meets specified conditions.

For more information about transitional policies, see http://www.cms. gov/CCIIO/Resources/Regulations-and-Guidance/ Downloads/transition-to-compliant-policies-03-06-2015.pdf.

A number of ACA provisions focus on changing how insurers and sponsors of insurance (e.g., employers) offer coverage. Collectively, the market reforms establish federal minimum requirements regarding access to coverage, premiums,[4] benefits, cost-sharing,[5] and consumer protections while generally giving states the authority to enforce the reforms and the ability to expand on the reforms.[6] Some of the reforms apply to all three segments of the private insurance market (nongroup, small group, and large group), but many of the reforms focus specifically on the nongroup and small group insurance markets. These reforms are intended to address perceived failures in those markets, such as limited access to coverage and higher costs of coverage, and to provide some parity with the large group market, which may already have many of these features.

Some of the market reforms are new to certain insurance markets; others have been in place in some capacity due to either state or federal laws. For example, guaranteed issue is the requirement that an insurer accept every applicant for coverage as long as the applicant agrees to the terms and conditions of the insurance offer (e.g., the premium). In the early 1990s, some states passed laws requiring guaranteed issue in their small group markets, with fewer states adopting types of guaranteed issue laws in their nongroup markets.[7] In 1996, Congress passed the Health Insurance Portability and Accountability Act (HIPAA; P.L. 104-191), which requires guaranteed issue in the small group market in all states. The ACA extends these efforts by requiring, as of 2014, that all non-grandfathered nongroup and group plans (except those that are self-insured)[8] offer coverage on a guaranteed issue basis. However, not all plans are subject to these ACA market reforms (see "Exemptions from ACA Market Reforms" text box for further information).

Table 1 provides a brief overview of the market reforms in the ACA.

Table 1. Patient Protection and Affordable Care Act (ACA) Private Health Insurance Market Reforms

ACA Provision	Brief Description
Obtaining Health Insurance	
Extension of dependent coverage	Applicable plans that offer dependent coverage must make that coverage available to children under the age of 26.
Prohibition of discrimination based on salary	Applicable plans are prohibited from establishing eligibility criteria for full-time employees based on salary.
Guaranteed issue	Applicable plans are required to accept every applicant for health coverage (as long as the applicant agrees to the terms and conditions of the insurance offer).
Nondiscrimination based on health status	Applicable plans are prohibited from basing eligibility for coverage on health status-related factors.
Waiting period limitation	Applicable plans cannot establish a waiting period of more than 90 days.
Maintaining Health Insurance	
Prohibition on rescissions	Applicable plans are prohibited from rescinding coverage except in cases of fraud or intentional misrepresentation.
Guaranteed renewability	Applicable plans must renew individual coverage at the option of the policyholder or group coverage at the option of the plan sponsor.
Cost of Purchasing Health Insurance	
Review of "unreasonable" rate increases	Applicable plans must submit a justification for an "unreasonable" rate increase to the Secretary of Health and Human Services (HHS) and the relevant state prior to implementation of the increase.
Rating restrictions	Applicable plans can only adjust premiums based on certain ACA-specified factors.
Covered Benefits	
Coverage of preventive health services with no cost-sharing	Applicable plans are required to provide coverage for preventive health services without cost-sharing.

Table 1. (Continued)

ACA Provision	Brief Description
Coverage of preexisting health conditions	Applicable plans are prohibited from excluding coverage for preexisting health conditions for all individuals.
Limits on Cost-Sharing	
Prohibition on lifetime limits	Applicable plans are prohibited from imposing lifetime limits on the dollar value of the essential health benefits (EHB).
Prohibition on annual limits	Applicable plans are prohibited from imposing annual limits on the dollar value of the EHB.
Other Consumer Protections	
Medical loss ratio requirement	Applicable plans are required to spend a certain amount of premium revenue on medical claims or otherwise provide rebates to policyholders.
Standardized appeals process	Applicable plans must implement an effective appeals process for coverage determinations and claims.
Patient protections	Applicable plans must comply with requirements related to choice of health care professionals and benefits for emergency services.
Summary of benefits and coverage	Applicable plans must provide a summary of benefits and coverage to individuals that meets the requirements specified by the HHS Secretary.
Reporting requirements regarding quality of care	Applicable plans must annually submit reports to the HHS Secretary and enrollees that address plan quality.
Nondiscrimination regarding clinical trial participation	Applicable plans cannot prohibit enrollees from participating in approved clinical trials.
Nondiscrimination regarding health care providers	Applicable plans are not allowed to discriminate, with respect to participation under the plan, against health care providers acting within the scope of their license or certification.

Source: Congressional Research Service (CRS) analysis of the ACA and its implementing regulations.

Essential Health Benefits Package

Both state and federal governments have the authority to require private plans to comply with specified rules and regulations, such as offering certain benefits and services. The ACA includes a provision that expands federal requirements with regard to covered benefits and cost-sharing structures. The ACA requires that all non-grandfathered plans offered in the nongroup and small group markets (both inside and outside exchanges) offer the essential health benefits (EHB).

The ACA does not explicitly define the EHB; rather, it lists 10 broad categories from which benefits and services must be included[9] and requires the Secretary of Health and Human Services (HHS) to further define the EHB. For 2014 and 2015, [10] the HHS Secretary asked states to select a benchmark plan from four different types of plans.[11] Plans that are required to offer the EHB must model their benefits package after the state's benchmark plan.[12] Plans must supplement their benchmark plans to ensure that benefits and services from all 10 statutorily required categories are represented.

The EHB package includes limits on enrollees' cost-sharing requirements. The ACA specifies that the limits work in two[13] ways: they prohibit (1) applying deductibles to preventive health services and (2) annual out-of-pocket limits that exceed existing limits in the tax code.[14] In 2015, the limit is $6,600 for an individual plan and $13,200 for a family plan.

The ACA and Actuarial Value

Actuarial value is a summary measure of a plan's generosity of coverage, expressed as a percentage of medical expenses for a standard population and a set of allowed charges estimated to be paid by the issuer. In other words, actuarial values reflect the relative proportions of cost-sharing that may be imposed. On average, the lower the actuarial value of a plan, the greater the cost-sharing for the enrollee.

However, because actuarial value is a summary measure based on a standard population, it is of varying value to individuals. Its value for an individual depends on how the individual's medical costs align with the costs of the standard population. Actuarial value also does not take into account aspects of health insurance coverage that may be important to individuals. In particular, it does not consider the cost of premiums and the adequacy of provider networks, and plans with the same actuarial value do not necessarily include the same set of covered benefits.

Additionally, plans offering the EHB package must meet one of four levels of generosity of coverage based on actuarial value. (See "ACA and Actuarial Value" text box for more information.)

The ACA requires plans that offer the EHB package to meet one of four generosity levels (*metal tiers*):

- bronze—60% actuarial value;
- silver—70% actuarial value;
- gold—80% actuarial value; and
- platinum—90% actuarial value.

INDIVIDUAL MANDATE

As of January 1, 2014, ACA requires that most individuals maintain health insurance coverage or pay a penalty for noncompliance. To comply with the individual mandate, most individuals need to obtain *minimum essential coverage*, which includes most types of private (e.g., employer-sponsored insurance and nongroup coverage) and public coverage (e.g., Medicare and Medicaid). Certain individuals are exempt from the mandate, including those with qualifying religious exemptions; those whose household income is less than the filing threshold for federal income taxes for the applicable tax year; those whose required contribution for self-only coverage for a calendar year exceeds 8% of household income;[15] those who receive a hardship exemption from the HHS Secretary; and those who are not lawfully present in the United States.

The individual mandate is often described as working in conjunction with certain ACA market reform, including guaranteed issue and renewability, nondiscrimination based on health status, coverage of preexisting health conditions, and rating restrictions (see *Table 1*). Collectively, these reforms require insurers to accept all applicants and concurrently restrict insurers' ability to vary premiums based on an applicant's health status and other characteristics. Because these reforms attempt to provide improved access to coverage for sick individuals or those at high risk of becoming ill, many argue that a provision such as the individual mandate is necessary to encourage healthy individuals to participate in the market so insurer risk pools are not limited to individuals who are high users of health care services (e.g., individuals who have multiple medical conditions).

Individuals are required to pay a penalty for each month of noncompliance with the mandate (provided they are not exempt from the mandate). The annual penalty is the *greater* of a percentage of "applicable income"[16] or a flat dollar amount assessed on each taxpayer and any dependents. *Table 2* provides the percentage of applicable income and flat dollar penalty amounts for 2014-2016. After 2016, the penalty will be adjusted for inflation.

Table 2. Individual Mandate Penalty

Year	Percentage of Applicable Income	Flat Dollar Amount
2014	1.0%	$95
2015	2.0%	$325
2016	2.5%	$695

Source: CRS analysis of the Patient Protection and Affordable Care Act (ACA; P.L. 111-148) and its implementing regulations.

Notes: Penalty will be adjusted for inflation after 2016. The ACA caps the penalty for noncompliance; the penalty in any given year cannot exceed the national average premium for bronze-level coverage offered through exchanges (for the relevant family size).

Taxpayers who are required to pay a penalty but fail to do so will receive a notice from the Internal Revenue Service (IRS) stating that they owe the penalty. If they still do not pay the penalty, the IRS can attempt to collect the funds by reducing the amount of the taxpayers' tax refund for that year or future years. However, individuals who fail to pay the penalty will not be subject to any criminal prosecution or penalty for such failure. The Secretary of the Treasury cannot file notice of lien or a levy on any property for a taxpayer who does not pay the penalty.

EXCHANGES (MARKETPLACES)

The ACA requires the establishment of a health insurance exchange (*marketplace*) in every state as of January 1, 2014. ACA exchanges are marketplaces in which individuals and small businesses can shop for and purchase private health insurance coverage.[17] To facilitate the purchase of insurance by these groups, the ACA requires the exchanges to have two parts: an exchange in which individuals can buy nongroup insurance for themselves and their families (an individual exchange) and a small business health options program (SHOP) exchange that is designed to assist qualified small employers and their employees with the purchase of insurance.

Exchanges are intended to simplify the experience of providing and obtaining coverage. They are not intended to supplant the private market outside of exchanges. The ACA requires that plans offered through an exchange are, for the most part, qualified health plans (QHPs). In general, to be a QHP, a plan has to offer the EHB package and meet certain standards related to marketing, choice of providers, and plan networks.[18] Each exchange is responsible for certifying the plans it offers.

Individual Exchange and Financial Assistance

The individual exchange is among the ACA provisions directed at the nongroup market. The ACA requires that each state establish an individual health insurance exchange. A state may set up its own exchange or create an exchange in partnership with the federal government. All health plans available through the nongroup exchanges must meet certain federally required criteria, such as offering the EHBs.

The open enrollment period for 2015 coverage through the individual exchange is November 15, 2014 to February 15, 2015. Individuals enrolled in a 2014 exchange plan can renew their current health plan or choose a new health plan through the exchange during the 2015 open enrollment period. However, if an individual enrolled in a 2014 exchange plan did not make any changes to his or her coverage by December 15, 2014, that individual was automatically reenrolled in the same health plan he or she selected in 2014.[19]

Individuals purchasing nongroup coverage through the exchange may be eligible to receive financial assistance. Financial assistance for obtaining coverage is based on income and provided through premium tax credits and cost-sharing subsidies.

Premium Tax Credits

Premium tax credits are generally available to individuals who

- are a part of a tax-filing unit;
- purchase nongroup coverage through an exchange;
- have household income[20] at or above 100%[21] of the federal poverty level (FPL)[22] but not more than 400% FPL;[23]
- are not eligible for minimum essential coverage;[24] and
- are U.S. citizens (or legally residing in the United States).

Although the tax credits are generally directed at individuals who do not have access to coverage outside the nongroup market, certain individuals with access to employer-sponsored insurance (ESI) may be eligible for premium tax credits. An individual eligible for ESI may still be eligible for premium credits if the employer's coverage either is deemed unaffordable[25] or does not provide minimum value.[26] If this were the case, the individual could purchase nongroup coverage through an exchange with the assistance of a premium tax credit.[27]

The premium credits established under the ACA are advanceable and refundable, meaning tax filers need not wait until the end of the tax year to benefit from the credit and may claim the full credit amount even if they have little or no federal income tax liability. The amount of the premium tax credit varies from person to person. The credit is based on the household income of the tax filer (and dependents), the premium for the exchange plan in which the tax filer (and dependents) is enrolled, and other factors.

The amounts received in premium credits are based on the household's prior year's income tax returns or estimates of household income for the current year. These amounts are reconciled in the next year when individuals file tax returns for the actual year in which they receive premium credits. If a tax filing unit's income decreases during the tax year and the filer should have received a larger tax credit, this additional credit amount will be included in the tax refund for that year. Any excess amount that was overpaid in premium credits will have to be repaid to the federal government as a tax payment. The ACA limits the amount of required repayments for lower-income enrollees. [28]

Cost-Sharing Subsidies

Under the ACA, some individuals will also be eligible to receive financial assistance in the form of cost-sharing subsidies that go toward cost-sharing expenses, such as deductibles, coinsurance, and co-payments. To be eligible, individuals must be eligible for premium tax credits and enrolled in a nongroup silver plan through an exchange.[29]

Cost-sharing assistance is provided in two forms, and both forms are based on income. Some individuals may receive both types of cost-sharing subsidies if they meet the applicable eligibility requirements. The first form of cost-sharing assistance reduces the annual out-of-pocket limits for individuals with income between 100% FPL and 250% FPL.[30] The second form, which also applies to individuals with income between 100% FPL and 250% FPL, involves reducing eligible individuals' cost-sharing requirements to ensure that the plans in which they have enrolled cover a certain percentage of allowed health care expenses, on average. This form of cost-sharing assistance directly affects cost-sharing requirements, such as deductibles, coinsurance, and co-payments.

Small Business Health Options Program Exchange

The small business health option program (SHOP) exchanges are among the ACA provisions directed at the small group market. SHOP exchanges are marketplaces in which private health insurance issuers sell health insurance plans to small employers. Like the individual exchanges, all health plans available through SHOP exchanges must meet certain federally required criteria, such as offering the EHB.

Small employers that offer health insurance coverage to all of their full-time employees are eligible to use the SHOP exchange.[31] Prior to January 1, 2016, the ACA allows states to define a small employer as having either 100 or fewer employees or 50 or fewer employees.[32] In 2016, all states must define a small employer as having 100 or fewer employees. In 2017, states will have the option to allow large employers to use the SHOP exchange.

Small Business Tax Credit

The ACA includes provisions whereby certain small employers may be eligible for a tax credit, provided they contribute at least 50% toward their employees' health insurance premiums. The small business health insurance tax credit is generally available to qualifying nonprofit and for-profit employers with fewer than 25 full-time equivalent (FTE) employees with average annual wages that fall under a statutorily specified cap.[33]

Small employers can claim the *full* credit amount if they meet the following two criteria:

- The employer has 10 or fewer FTEs.
- The employer's average taxable wages are $25,400 or less in 2014 (adjusted for inflation in subsequent years). This figure is calculated by dividing the aggregate amount of wages paid to employees during the year by the number of FTEs (and then rounding to the nearest $1,000).

In 2014, the credit was phased out as the number of FTEs increased from 10 FTEs to 25 FTEs and as average employee compensation increased from $25,400 to $50,800.[34] The full credit in 2014 covered up to 50% of the for-profit employer's contribution and 35% of the nonprofit employer's contribution. From 2014 onward, the credit is only available to an employer for two consecutive tax years and to employers who obtain coverage through a SHOP exchange.[35]

EMPLOYER REQUIREMENTS AND PENALTIES RELATED TO THE OFFER OF INSURANCE

Certain large employers are subject to a *shared responsibility* provision. This provision does not explicitly mandate that a large employer offer employees health insurance; instead, it has the potential to impose penalties on large employers that do not provide affordable and adequate coverage to their full-time employees (and those employee's dependents).

The ACA includes an employer penalty that was to be imposed in 2014. However, based on guidance issued by the IRS, the penalty will not be assessed until 2015. The employer requirements and penalty is being phased in—the requirement applies to large firms with 100 or more FTE employees in 2015 and employers with 50 or more FTE employees in 2016.[36]

A large employer, regardless of the offer of coverage, may be subject to a penalty if any of its full-time employees[37] obtain coverage through an exchange and receive a premium tax credit. Calculation of the penalty amount depends on whether the employer offers coverage and the total number of full-time employees working for the employer. Large employers that offer coverage will only have to pay a penalty if a full-time employee receives a premium tax credit. An employee will receive a premium tax credit only if his or her self-only coverage from the employer either exceeds 9.5% of household income or pays for less than 60%, on average, of covered health care expenses. Large employers that do not offer coverage may be subject to a penalty only if at least one full-time employee receives a premium tax credit.

No employer may be subject to a penalty based upon health coverage for any part-time employee, even if the part-time employee receives a premium credit.

CONSUMER OPERATED AND ORIENTED PLAN PROGRAM

The ACA creates the Consumer Operated and Oriented Plan (CO-OP) program to foster nonprofit, member-run health insurance companies that would offer qualified health plans in the nongroup and small group markets. The HHS Secretary is required to use funds appropriated to the CO-OP program to finance start-up and solvency loans for eligible nonprofit organizations applying to become CO-OP issuers. Awarded entities are to use the start-up loans for assistance with costs associated with creating the CO-OP, and the solvency loans must be used to help the entity meet state solvency requirements.[38] All loans must be repaid with interest; the start-up loans must be repaid within 5 years and the solvency loans must be repaid within 15 years (from the date of disbursement).

As of the publication date of this report, 23 entities have received loans totaling over $2.1 billion.[39] As enacted, the ACA appropriated $6 billion of federal funds for the CO-OP program, but the American Taxpayer Relief Act of 2012 (ATRA; P.L. 112-240) rescinded most of the unobligated CO-OP funds. The funds remaining for the program must be used to support the 23 entities that have already received CO-OP loans.[40]

The entities that have received loans are required to meet certain standards with regard to the types of health plans they offer. Two-thirds of the plans offered by CO-OP issuers must be QHPs offered in the nongroup and small group markets; up to one-third of a CO-OP issuer's plans can be other types of plans, such as Medicaid managed care plans. With regard to how CO-OP issuers are expected to interact with exchanges, CO-OP plans must be offered at the silver and gold levels in the nongroup market in each exchange that serves the geographic regions in which the CO-OP loan recipient is licensed and intends to provide health care coverage. CO-OP plans must be offered at both the silver and gold levels in the small group market in each SHOP that serves the geographic regions in which the entity is offering coverage if the CO-OP loan recipient offers at least one plan in the small group market outside an exchange.

Multi-State Plan Program

To increase the number of plan choices offered through the exchanges, the ACA directs the Office of Personnel Management (OPM) to contract with private insurers in each state to offer at least two[41] comprehensive health insurance options, known as multi-state plans (MSPs). Some MSP options also offer in-network care for out-of-state services, but not all do. Individuals interested in MSP options would have access to the same financial assistance for premium tax credits and cost-sharing subsidies as enrollees in other plans.

OPM administers the contracts in a similar manner as the Federal Employee Health Benefits Program (FEHBP). This includes negotiating plan benefits, monitoring performance, and overseeing compliance with ACA provisions. MSPs must cover the EHBs and comply with ACA cost-sharing limits. Carriers must be licensed in each state and comply with state laws. Because the EHBs differ among states, MSPs can choose to follow a particular state's EHB package or one of the three largest by enrollment FEHBP packages.

OPM can contract with a health insurance issuer to offer an MSP if the health insurance issuer agrees to a phase-in expansion. MSPs would have to be made available in 35 states by 2015, 43 states in 2016 and 2017, and all states by open enrollment in 2017.

In 2014, OPM contracted with the Blue Cross Blue Shield Association to offer over 150 MSPs in 30 states and the District of Columbia. For 2015, OPM has added a second group of insurers, an association of CO-OP programs, and the MSP program expanded to 5 additional states for a total of 36 states. The MSP program offers more than 200 plans on the exchanges for 2015.

State Options

Many of the provisions discussed to this point are required to be implemented under ACA. However, the ACA also includes provisions that states may choose to implement. The flexibility for states inherent in these *state option* provisions allows states to continue programs already in existence or create new programs that may be better-suited to their specific private insurance markets.

Basic Health Program

The ACA provides states an option to offer coverage to certain low-income individuals through a basic health program (BHP). Beginning in 2015,[42] states are able to establish a BHP, which is a health insurance program for individuals under the age of 65 who are not eligible for Medicaid or eligible to enroll in minimum essential coverage. A BHP is offered in lieu of these individuals obtaining coverage through an exchange. The BHP is available to individuals with household income between 133% FPL[43] and 200% FPL,[44] and the BHP coverage must be at least as comprehensive and affordable as what the individuals could have obtained through an exchange. A state that chooses to establish a BHP will receive some funds from the federal government to operate the program.[45]

As of the publication date of this report, CMS approved MinnesotaCare as the nation's first BHP, after Minnesota became the first state to win approval for this option under the ACA.

Waiver for State Innovation

The ACA allows a state to apply to the HHS Secretary for a waiver of specific requirements with respect to health insurance coverage within that state for plan years beginning on or after January 1, 2017. The state may apply to waive any or all of the following:

- requirements relating to the establishment of QHPs;
- requirement for the state to have an exchange;
- requirement to offer premium tax credits and cost-sharing reductions through an exchange;
- requirement for individuals to maintain coverage (individual mandate); and
- penalties imposed on employers whose employees receive premium tax credits.

For a state to obtain a waiver, the HHS Secretary and the Secretary of the Treasury need sufficient information from the state to determine that its proposed waiver will provide benefits that are at least as comprehensive as the EHBs; provide coverage and cost-sharing protections against excessive out-of-pocket spending that are at least as affordable as the cost-sharing provisions in the ACA; provide coverage to at least a comparable number of residents as the provisions of the ACA that affect private health insurance would provide; and not increase the federal deficit.

Health Care Choice Compacts

The ACA allows two or more states to create a health care choice compact. The compact would allow the states to enter into an agreement whereby one or more QHPs could be offered in the nongroup market in all states in the compact. In this arrangement, a QHP would only be subject to the laws and regulations of the state in which the plan was issued; however, the issuer of such QHP would be subject to other rules and requirements (e.g., market conduct rules, consumer protection rules) imposed by the state(s) in which the consumer resides. Additionally, the issuer would either be required to be licensed in each state in the compact or to submit to each state's standards for offering insurance, and the issuer would have to notify all consumers that it may not comply with their state's rules.

A state must have a law that specifically authorizes it to enter into a compact. The HHS Secretary may approve a compact if the agreement meets certain requirements. The ACA directed the HHS Secretary to promulgate regulations on this provision no later than July 31, 2013; as of the publication date of this report, the regulations have not been promulgated. Approved compacts cannot go into effect before January 1, 2016.

RISK MITIGATION PROGRAMS

As part of a larger set of private health insurance market reforms, beginning in 2014, the ACA requires private health insurance issuers to provide coverage to individuals regardless of health status, medical history, and preexisting conditions. Some individuals are eligible to receive premium tax credits and cost-sharing subsidies through an exchange (marketplace), which can increase the attractiveness of coverage by reducing its cost. The individual mandate is also in effect, which requires most individuals to maintain coverage or otherwise pay a penalty.

All the new health insurance market reforms and the expanded market of individuals seeking to purchase insurance contribute to the uncertainty insurers face as they try to price their insurance products in the first few years of the ACA's implementation. Additional questions insurers face include: Will young and healthy uninsured individuals purchase insurance? Have individuals who were previously uninsured been delaying necessary health care, and how much will their health care utilization (and costs) change when they have insurance? How many employers will send their employees to the exchanges to acquire insurance? How will competitors in the market price their products?

The ACA establishes *three* programs to help mitigate the financial risk insurers face as a result of the insurance market reforms. The *risk adjustment program* is a permanent program that began in 2014 and is intended to mitigate the effects of adverse selection both inside and outside of the new exchanges. Adverse selection occurs when individuals who expect or plan for high use of health services enroll in more generous and often more expensive health plans and, simultaneously, individuals who expect or plan for low use of health services enroll in more modest plans (both in terms of price and benefits) or choose not to enroll in coverage. Adverse selection can thus lead to insurers *enrolling* either a large number of high-cost individuals or a disproportionate number of low-cost individuals, depending on plan offerings. Risk adjustment is an adjustment to plan *payments* to reflect the higher cost of enrolling a relatively sicker group of enrollees or the lower cost of enrolling a relatively healthier group of enrollees.

The ACA also establishes two temporary programs to help mitigate other types of plan risks. The *reinsurance program* is a temporary program (2014-2016) designed to compensate plans for the cost of individual enrollees who have excessively high medical expenses, such as those who may have delayed receiving needed health care. The *risk corridor program* is a temporary program (2014-2016) designed to mitigate excessive losses (or gains) that result from errors in estimating premiums as the new market reforms get under way. See *Table 3* for more information about the risk programs.

Table 3. Description of the Patient Protection and Affordable Care Act (ACA) Risk Mitigation Programs

	Reinsurance	Risk Corridors	Risk Adjustment
Goal	Offset a plan's risk associated with high-cost enrollees.	Protect against inaccurate rate setting.	Protect against adverse selection.[a]
Objective	Provide funding to plans that incur high costs for individual enrollees.	Limit the issuers' losses (and gains).	Transfer funds from lowest-risk plans to highest-risk plans.
Description	Reinsurance typically is thought of as insurance for insurers. When issuing policies, an insurer faces the risk that the premiums[b] it collects will not be sufficient to cover its expenses and generate profit. Reinsurance shifts the risk of covering high expenses from the primary insurer to a reinsurer. The ACA requires all health insurance issuers and third-party administrators of	Risk corridors refer to a mechanism that adjusts payments[c] to health plans according to a formula based on each plan's actual, allowed expenses in relation to a target amount. If a plan's expenses exceed a certain percentage above the target, the plan's payment is increased. Likewise, if a plan's expenses are	Risk adjustment refers to a mechanism that adjusts payments to health plans to take into account the risk that each plan is bearing based on its enrollee population. Plans with enrollment of less-than-average risk will pay an assessment to the state.

	Reinsurance	Risk Corridors	Risk Adjustment
	group health plans (including self-insured plans) to contribute to a reinsurance program administered by a nonprofit reinsurance entity. The contribution rate for 2015 is $44 per covered life. Non-grandfathered individual market plans (inside and outside of exchanges) are eligible for payments from the reinsurance program.	at least a certain percentage below the target, the plan's payment is decreased. Under the ACA, HHS must make payments to a QHP issuer that experiences losses greater than 3% of the issuer's projections, whereas a QHP issuer whose gains are greater than 3% of its projections must remit payments to HHS. All QHPs in the individual and small group markets (inside and outside of exchanges) must participate in the risk corridor.	States will provide payments to plans with higher-than-average risk. All non-grandfathered individual and small group market plans (inside and outside the exchanges) are subject to risk adjustment.
Time Frame	Three years (2014-2016)	Three years (2014-2016)	Permanent; began after end of benefit year 2014

Source: CRS analysis of the ACA and its implementing regulations.

Notes: HHS = Department of Health and Human Services. QHP = qualified health plan.

[a] Adverse selection occurs when individuals who expect or plan for high use of health services tend to enroll in more generous (and consequently more expensive) health plans.

[b] Premiums refer, in general, to payments from an insured individual to the issuer.

[c] In this table, payments are between the insurer and HHS Secretary, either to or from.

End Notes

[1] What constitutes large and small in the private market varies. Often, for the purpose of state and federal laws, a large employer has 50 or more employees and a small employer has up to 50 employees. The definitions of small and large also vary under the Patient Protection and Affordable Care Act (ACA; P.L. 111-148, as amended), but most often the ACA defines small as either up to 50 or up to 100 employees.

[2] U.S. Census Bureau, Current Population Survey, "Health Insurance Coverage in the United States: 2013," September 2014, available at http://www.census.gov/content/dam/Census/library/publications/2014/demo/p60-250.pdf.

[3] The intent of health insurance is to minimize the potential financial risk associated with use of health care services. One way to minimize risk in the insurance market is to spread risk among a group of people. This concept is often called risk pooling. A group of individuals contributes to a common pool (risk pool), and contributions from low-cost individuals in the pool (i.e., individuals who use few medical services) subsidize the medical costs of higher-cost individuals in the pool.

[4] A premium is the amount paid for health insurance, often on a monthly basis.

[5] Cost-sharing is the share of costs an insured individual pays for services; the term often includes deductibles, coinsurance, and co-payments. A deductible is the amount an insured individual pays before his or her health insurance issuer begins to pay for services. Coinsurance is the share of costs, figured in percentage form, an insured individual pays for a health service. A co-payment is a fixed amount an insured individual pays for a health service.

[6] Private health insurance is primarily regulated at the state level. The ACA establishes uniform requirements and additional options for all states.

[7] Mila Kofman and Karen Pollitz, Health Insurance Regulation by States and the Federal Government: A Review of Current Approaches and Proposals for Change, Georgetown University Health Policy Institute, April 2006.

[8] A common distinction in the group market is whether plans are fully insured or self-insured. A fully insured plan is one in which the insurer or insurance sponsor purchases health coverage and the insurer assumes the risk of providing health benefits to the sponsor's enrolled members. A self-insured plan is one in which an entity (e.g., employer or association) provides coverage for its members directly by setting aside funds and paying for health benefits. Under self-insurance, the entity bears the risk for covering medical expenses, and self-insured plans are not subject to state insurance regulations.

[9] The 10 categories are ambulatory patient services; emergency services; hospitalization; maternity and newborn care; mental health and substance use disorder services, including behavioral health treatment; prescription drugs; rehabilitative and habilitative services and devices; laboratory services; preventive and wellness services and chronic disease management; and pediatric services, including oral and vision care.

[10] As of the publication date of this report, final 2016 guidance for the essential health benefits has not been released.

[11] 78 Federal Register 12834, February 25, 2013.

[12] Summaries of each state's selected benchmark plan are available at http://www.cms.gov/CCIIO/Resources/DataResources/ehb.html.

[13] The ACA previously limited cost-sharing in three ways. It also included deductible limits for plans offered in the small group market—generally prohibiting these plans from having deductibles greater than $2,000 for self-only coverage and $4,000 for any other coverage in 2014. However, the Protecting Access to Medicare Act of 2014 (P.L. 113-93) repealed this provision, thereby removing the limitation on deductibles for plans offered in the small group market.

[14] The existing limits are those that are applicable to high-deductible health plans that qualify to be paired with health savings accounts. For more information on consumer-driven health care, see CRS Report RL32237, Health Insurance: A Primer.

[15] After 2014, the 8% will be adjusted to reflect the excess rate of premium growth above the rate of income growth for the period. In 2015, the required contribution for self-only coverage must exceed 8.05% of household income.

[16] "Applicable income" is defined as the amount by which an individual's household income exceeds the applicable filing threshold for the applicable tax year.

[17] Individuals who approach exchanges could also potentially be screened for eligibility for public programs such as Medicaid and the State Children's Health Insurance Program (CHIP).

[18] For more information about the types of plans offered through exchanges, see CRS Report R43233, Private Health Plans Under the ACA: In Brief.

[19] The individual's coverage will be renewed in the same plan as his or her current plan, unless the current plan is unavailable. These individuals can also select a plan between December 16, 2014 and February 15, 2015, but the plan selection will not be effective for January 1, 2015 coverage. For additional information, see 45 C.F.R. § 155.335.

[20] In this instance, household income is modified adjust gross income.

[21] Lawfully present immigrants with income below 100% of the federal poverty line (FPL), who are ineligible for Medicaid for the first five years that they are present in the United States, are also eligible for premium tax credits. For the purpose of the credits, these individuals will be treated as though their income were exactly 100% FPL.

[22] The guidelines that designate the federal poverty level are used in a variety of federal programs for eligibility purposes. The poverty guidelines vary by family size and by whether the individual resides in the 48 contiguous states and the District of Columbia, Alaska, or Hawaii. Office of the Assistant Secretary for Planning and Evaluation, "Frequently Asked Questions Related to the Poverty Guidelines and Poverty," http://aspe.hhs.gov/Poverty/faq.cfm#programs.

[23] For 2015, the income range corresponding with 100% FPL and 400% FPL is $11,670-$46,680 for a single individual and $23,850-$95,400 for a family of four. FPL amounts are higher in Alaska and Hawaii.

[24] The types of coverage that have been statutorily designated as minimum essential coverage include government-sponsored programs, employer-sponsored plans, plans in the individual market, and grandfathered health plans. 45 C.F.R. § 156.604.

[25] Affordable in this context means the individual's required contribution toward the plan premium for self-only coverage does not exceed 9.5% of his or her household income.

[26] Minimum value in this context means the plan pays for at least 60%, on average, of covered health care expenses.

[27] In this scenario, the individual's employer could be subject to a penalty. See "Employer Requirements and Penalties Related to the Offer of Insurance."

[28] The caps have been modified a few times since the ACA's enactment. For more information, see CRS Report R41137, Health Insurance Premium Credits in the Patient Protection and Affordable Care Act (ACA).

[29] The ACA establishes different cost-sharing subsidy eligibility criteria for American Indians and Alaskan Natives. For more information, see CRS Report R41152, Indian Health Care: Impact of the Affordable Care Act (ACA).

[30] In 2015, the annual limit is $6,600 for an individual plan and $13,200 for a family plan.

[31] An employer's Small Business Health Options Program (SHOP) exchange eligibility depends on size and whether the employer offers coverage to all full-time employees. ACA and its implementing regulations set forth methods and definitions with respect to determining employer size and whether an employee is full time. For more information about the

definitions and methods employers must use to determine size, see CRS Report R43771, Small Business Health Options Program (SHOP) Exchange.

[32] According to a March 2014 report published by the Commonwealth Fund, all states chose the 50-employee limit for 2014. See the Commonwealth Fund, Implementing the Affordable Care Act: State Action to Establish SHOP Marketplaces, March 2014.

[33] Full-time equivalent employees (FTEs) are calculated by dividing the total hours worked by all employees during the tax year by 2,080 (with a maximum of 2,080 hours for any one employee). For calculating the number of FTEs and their wages, the term employee includes all individuals who are considered employees under the common law standard, including those who do not work full time. However, the term excludes seasonal workers (persons working no more than 120 days during the year). In addition, the term excludes self-employed individuals, 2% shareholders in an S-corporation, 5% owners of an eligible small business, and anyone who is a relation or dependent of these people.

[34] The amounts will be adjusted for inflation using the Consumer Price Index-Urban in subsequent years.

[35] The Internal Revenue Service (IRS) provides transition relief for certain small employers that cannot obtain a qualified health plan (QHP) offered through a SHOP exchange because the small employer's principal business address is in a county in which a QHP through a SHOP was not available in 2014. The IRS has identified counties in Washington and Wisconsin to which this transition relief applies. See IRS Notice 2014-6 for more details.

[36] Generally, both full-time and part-time employees are included in the calculation to determine the number of FTEs the employer has, but the calculation does not include full-time seasonal employees who work for up to 120 days during the year.

[37] Full-time employees are those working 30 hours per week or more.

[38] States generally set standards for and monitor state-licensed insurers' financial operations to ensure that insurers have adequate reserves to pay policyholders' claims.

[39] One additional entity, an organization in Vermont, received Consumer Operated and Oriented Plan (CO-OP) loans, but the Centers for Medicare and Medicaid Services terminated the entity's loan agreement in 2013. For more information about the 23 loan recipients, see http://www.cms.gov/CCIIO/Resources/Grants/new-loan-program.html.

[40] The Department of Defense and Full-Year Continuing Appropriations Act, 2011 (P.L. 112-10) rescinded $2.2 billion of the appropriated funding, and the Consolidated Appropriations Act, 2012 (P.L. 112-74) rescinded an additional $400 million from the program. The American Taxpayer Relief Act of 2012 (ATRA; P.L. 112-240) rescinded nearly all other unobligated CO-OP funds. ATRA directed the Secretary of Health and Human Services (HHS) to create a fund to be used to support all nonprofit insurance issuers that were awarded CO-OP program loans prior to the date of the law's enactment (January 2, 2013). The fund contains 10% of any unobligated CO-OP funds, and the Act rescinded all other unobligated CO-OP funds.

[41] One of the issuers must be nonprofit.

[42] As enacted, the ACA allowed states to establish a Basic Health Program (BHP) beginning in 2014; however, HHS released guidance stating that the program will not be operational and available as a state option until 2015. For more information, see Questions and Answers: Medicaid and the Affordable Care Act, available at http://medicaid.gov/State-Resource-Center/FAQ-Medicaid-and-CHIP-Affordable-Care-Act-ACA-Implementation/Downloads/ACA-FAQ-BHP.pdf.

[43] The ACA includes a five percentage point income disregard, so the effective limit is 138% FPL.

[44] The BHP would also be available to individuals who are not citizens of the United States but are lawfully present and barred from Medicaid because of duration of U.S. residency. These individuals are eligible for a BHP if they otherwise meet the eligibility criteria and have household income not greater than 138% FPL.

[45] The ACA requires the HHS Secretary to transfer funds to a state that establishes a BHP in an amount equal to 95% of the premium tax credits and the cost-sharing reductions that would have been provided to the state's BHP enrollees had they been able to obtain coverage through an exchange.

In: Private-Sector Health Insurance
Editor: Stephen Maxwell Mathis
ISBN: 978-1-63483-772-9

Chapter 4

OVERVIEW OF HEALTH INSURANCE EXCHANGES*

Namrata K. Uberoi, Annie L. Mach and Bernadette Fernandez

SUMMARY

The Patient Protection and Affordable Care Act (ACA; P.L. 111-148, as amended) requires health insurance exchanges to be established in every state. Exchanges are marketplaces where individuals and small businesses can shop for and purchase private health insurance coverage. States must have two types of exchanges; an individual exchange and a small business health options program (SHOP) exchange.

Exchanges may be established either by the state itself as a state-based exchange (SBE) or by the Secretary of Health and Human Services (HHS) as a federally-facilitated exchange (FFE). In states with FFEs, the exchange may be operated solely by the federal government or in conjunction with the state.

Persons who obtain coverage through the individual exchange may be eligible for financial assistance from the federal government. The financial assistance in the individual exchanges is available in two forms: premium tax credits and cost-sharing subsidies. Small businesses that use

* This is an edited, reformatted and augmented version of a Congressional Research Service publication R44065, prepared for Members and Committees of Congress, dated June 30, 2015

the SHOP exchange may be eligible for small business health insurance tax credits. The tax credits assist small businesses with the cost of providing health insurance coverage to employees.

The ACA generally requires that health insurance plans offered through an exchange are Qualified Health Plans (QHPs). Typically in order to be a certified as a QHP, a plan must offer the essential health benefits, comply with cost-sharing limits, and meet certain market reforms. Exchanges may also offer other types of health insurance plans such as catastrophic and dental-only plans.

This report provides an overview of the various components of the health insurance exchanges. The report includes summary information about how exchanges are structured, the intended consumers for health insurance exchange plans, and consumer assistance available in the exchanges, as specified in the ACA. The report also describes the availability of financial assistance for certain exchange consumers and small businesses and outlines the range of plans offered through exchanges. Moreover, the report provides a brief summary of the implementation and operation of exchanges in 2014 and 2015.

INTRODUCTION

The Patient Protection and Affordable Care Act (ACA; P.L. 111-148, as amended) requires health insurance exchanges (also known as *marketplaces*) to be established in every state. ACA exchanges are marketplaces in which individuals and small businesses can shop for and purchase private health insurance coverage. Exchanges are intended to simplify the experience of providing and obtaining health insurance. They are not intended to supplant the private market outside of the exchanges but to provide an additional source of private health insurance coverage.

This report provides an overview of the various components of the health insurance exchanges. The report includes summary information about how exchanges are structured, the intended consumers for health insurance exchange plans, and consumer assistance available in the exchanges, as specified in the ACA. The report also describes the availability of financial assistance for certain exchange consumers and small businesses and outlines the range of plans offered through exchanges. Moreover, the report provides a brief summary of the implementation and operation of exchanges in 2014 and 2015.

EXCHANGE STRUCTURE AND OPERATION

The ACA required health insurance exchanges to be established in all states. These health insurance exchanges were in operation in October 2013 to allow consumers to shop for health insurance plans that began as soon as January 1, 2014. ACA exchanges are marketplaces in which individuals and small businesses can shop for and purchase private health insurance coverage. Each state has two types of exchanges—an *individual exchange*[1] and a *small business health options program (SHOP) exchange*. An individual exchange is where individuals can purchase nongroup insurance and apply for premium and cost-sharing subsidies. A SHOP exchange is where small businesses can purchase small-group insurance and apply for small business health insurance tax credits. These exchanges may be operated under the same or separate governing structures. In this report, the use of the term *exchange* without the qualifier of *individual* or *SHOP* refers to both types of exchanges.

A state can choose to establish its own state-based exchange (SBE). If a state opts not to, or if the Department of Health and Human Services (HHS) determines that the state is not in a position to administer its own exchange, then HHS will establish and administer the exchange in the state as a federally-facilitated exchange (FFE).

There are varying levels of state involvement in FFEs. In many states with FFEs, the exchange is wholly operated and administered by HHS. In some cases, states may partner with HHS to establish and administer the exchange. For the 2015 coverage year, 34 states have FFEs, 13 states and the District of Columbia have SBEs, and 3 states have SBEs but use the federal information technology (IT) platform (i.e., HealthCare.gov) (see *Figure 1*).

Moreover, HHS may administer the individual exchange while the state administers the SHOP exchange. For the 2015 coverage year, most states have the same entity administer both the individual and SHOP exchanges (see *Figure 1*). However, two states—Mississippi and Utah— elected to administer their SHOP exchanges while HHS administers their individual exchanges (see *Figure 1*).

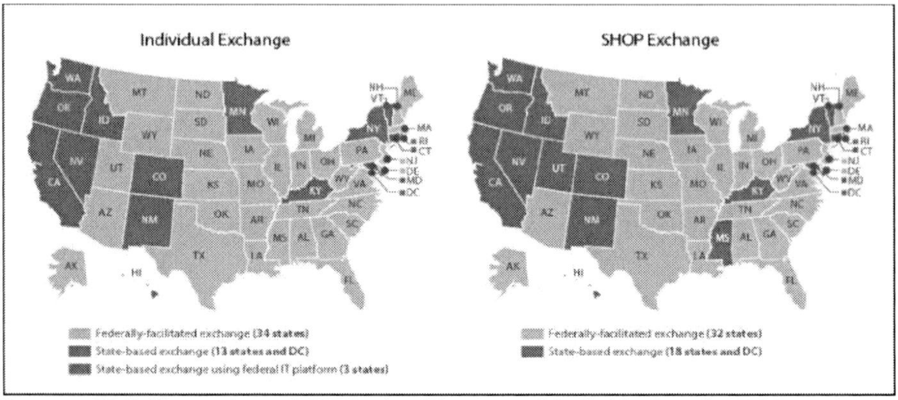

Source: CRS illustration of HHS classification of individual and SHOP exchange types. Note: SHOP is the small business health options program.

Figure 1. Individual and SHOP Exchange Types by State, 2015.

Exchange Consumer Assistance

Statute and regulations require that exchanges carry out certain consumer assistance functions. Some functions require that exchanges provide direct support to consumers. For example, exchanges must provide for the operation of a call center that addresses the needs of consumers who have questions about individual exchanges and SHOP exchanges.

Exchanges are also expected to provide indirect support to consumers by implementing consumer assistance personnel programs. Exchanges must establish Navigator programs and certified application counselor programs, and exchanges have the option to implement a program for non-Navigator consumer assistance personnel. Under these programs, individuals are trained to help consumers make informed decisions about their insurance options and help consumers access individual and SHOP exchange coverage. However, consumer assistance personnel may not enroll individuals or small employers in coverage.

Pursuant to state law, exchanges may also allow insurance agents and brokers to help individuals and small employers obtain coverage through exchanges.[2] Unlike consumer assistance personnel, agents and brokers may enroll individuals and small employers in coverage through exchanges.

EXCHANGE FUNDING

The ACA provided an indefinite appropriation for HHS grants to states to support the planning and establishment of exchanges. For each fiscal year between FY2011 and FY2014, the HHS Secretary determined the total amount that was made available to each state for exchange grants.

None of the aforementioned exchange grants could be awarded after January 1, 2015, and exchanges were expected to be self-sustaining beginning in 2015. The ACA allows exchanges to generate funding to sustain their operations, including by assessing fees on participating health insurance plans. To raise funds for each of the FFEs, beginning in 2014, HHS is assessing a monthly fee on each health insurance plan that offers plans through a FFE.

EXCHANGE CONSUMERS

The ACA specifies that exchanges are established for the purpose of offering health plan options to individuals and small businesses.

Individuals

Individuals may enroll in plans through their states' exchanges as long as they (1) meet state residency requirements;[3] (2) are not incarcerated, except individuals in custody pending the disposition of charges; and (3) are U.S. citizens, U.S. nationals, or "lawfully present" residents.[4] Undocumented individuals are prohibited from purchasing coverage through the exchanges, even if they could pay the entire premium.

Individuals may purchase health insurance in the individual exchanges for themselves via individual plans or for their families via family plans.

Enrollment Periods

Individuals may enroll in exchange coverage only during specified enrollment periods. Most individuals enroll during the annual Open Enrollment Period (OEP). The next OEP, for 2016 exchange coverage, begins November 1, 2015, and ends on January 31, 2016. Individuals may also be allowed to enroll during a Special Enrollment Period (SEP). Individuals must qualify for enrollment during a SEP. Generally, this is due to a change in personal circumstances; for example, marriage or adoption. HHS may also establish SEPs for other circumstances, such as technical problems submitting insurance applications through the federal IT platform (i.e., HealthCare.gov).

Premium Tax Credits and Cost-Sharing Subsidies

Individuals purchasing coverage through the individual exchanges may be eligible to receive financial assistance. Eligibility for such assistance is based on income and provided in the form of premium tax credits and cost-sharing subsidies.

The premium tax credit is generally available to individuals who do not have access to subsidized public coverage (e.g., Medicaid) or employment-based coverage that meets certain standards.[5] The credit is designed to reduce an eligible individual's cost of purchasing health insurance coverage through the exchange. The credit itself is both advanceable and refundable, meaning tax filers need not wait until the end of the tax year to benefit from the credit and may claim the full credit amount even if they have little or no federal income tax liability. The amount of the premium tax credit varies from person to person. However, the credit is designed to provide larger credit amounts to individuals with lower incomes compared to those with higher incomes.

In addition to premium tax credits, certain individuals may also be eligible to receive subsidies that go toward cost-sharing expenses,[6] such as deductibles, coinsurance, and co-payments. Cost-sharing assistance is provided in two forms. The first form of assistance reduces the annual out-of-pocket limit applicable to a given exchange plan.[7] The second form reduces cost-sharing requirements applicable to a given exchange plan. Individuals may receive both types of cost-sharing subsidies if they meet the applicable eligibility requirements.

Small Businesses

Small businesses that offer health insurance coverage to all of their full-time employees are eligible to use SHOP exchanges. Prior to January 1, 2016, the ACA allows states to define *small* as businesses having either 100 or fewer or 50 or fewer employees. Beginning in 2016, all states must define *small* as businesses with 100 or fewer employees.[8] Beginning in 2017, states have the option to allow *large* businesses to use SHOP exchanges.

The small business must have its principal business in the SHOP exchange service area or offer coverage to each eligible employee through the SHOP exchange serving the employee's worksite. In order for an employee to be eligible to obtain coverage through a SHOP exchange, a SHOP-eligible employer must offer the employee coverage.

Enrollment Periods

Enrollment in a SHOP exchange is not limited to a specified open enrollment period except in certain circumstances.[9] Specific circumstances aside, a SHOP exchange must allow employers to enroll any time during a year, and the employer's plan year must consist of the 12-month period beginning with the employer's effective date of coverage.

Small Business Health Insurance Tax Credit

Under the ACA, certain small businesses are eligible for small business health insurance tax credits. In general, these credits are available only to small businesses that purchase coverage through SHOP exchanges. The intent of the credit is to assist small employers with the cost of providing health insurance coverage to employees. The credits are available to eligible small businesses for two consecutive tax years (beginning with the first year the small employer purchases coverage through a SHOP exchange).

The maximum credit is 50% of an employer's contribution toward premiums for for-profit employers, and 35% of employer contributions for nonprofit organizations. The full credit is available to employers that have 10 or fewer full-time equivalents (FTEs) and who have average taxable wages of $25,400 or less. For tax year 2015, the tax credit is phased out as an employer's number of FTEs increases from 10 to 25 and as average employee compensation increases from $25,800 to $51,600.

EXCHANGE PLANS

Qualified Health Plans

The ACA generally requires that health insurance plans offered through exchanges are Qualified Health Plans (QHPs). Typically in order to be a certified as a QHP a plan has to offer the essential health benefits (EHB), comply with cost-sharing limits, and meet certain market reforms. Each exchange is responsible for certifying the plans it offers. However, QHPs can be offered both inside the health insurance exchanges and outside the exchanges on the private health insurance market.

Essential Health Benefits

All QHPs are required to offer a core package of health care services, known as the essential health benefits. The ACA does not specifically define this core package but rather lists 10 benefit categories and requires the HHS Secretary to further define the EHB (see *Figure 2*).

For 2014-2016, the HHS Secretary outlined a process where each state identified a single plan, the EHB-benchmark plan, that serves as a reference plan for all QHPs in that state. Accordingly, QHPs must base their benefits package on their state's EHB-benchmark plan. Given that each state has its own EHB-benchmark plan and given other market factors, QHPs available in the health insurance exchanges will vary in terms of specific covered services as well as benefit amount, duration, and scope.

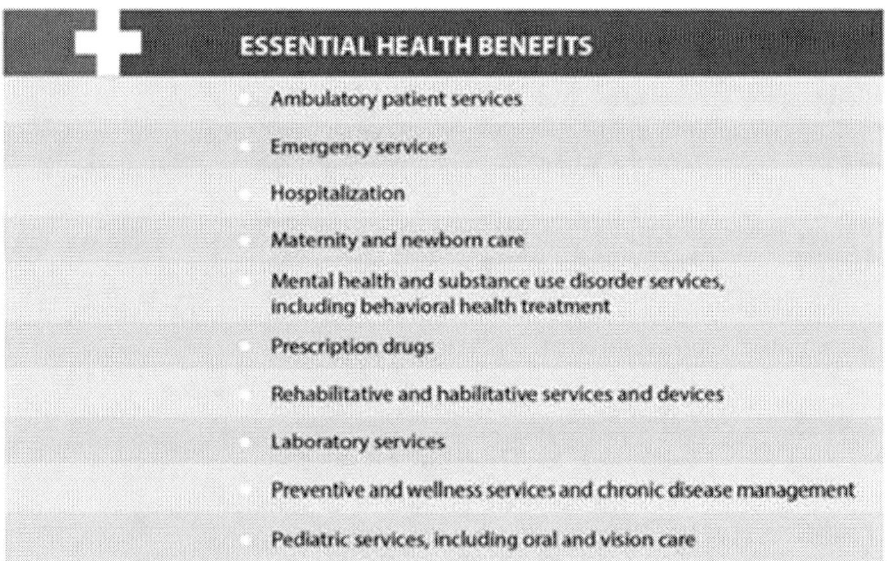

Source: 42 U.S.C. §18022.

Figure 2. The 10 Essential Health Benefits.

Cost-Sharing

QHPs must follow established limits on consumer cost-sharing. The ACA imposes limits on consumers' cost-sharing requirements for the EHB. The limits work in two ways: they prohibit (1) applying deductibles to preventive health services and (2) annual out-of-pocket limits that exceed existing limits in the federal tax code.[10] In 2015, the cost-sharing limit is $6,600 for an individual plan and $13,200 for a family plan. For 2016, the cost-sharing limit is $6,850 for an individual plan and $13,700 for a family plan.[11]

Actuarial Value

The ACA requires QHPs to tailor cost-sharing to comply with one of the four levels of actuarial value (AV) (see *Figure 3*). AV is a summary measure of a plan's generosity of coverage. It is expressed as the percentage a given health insurance plan will pay for covered medical expenses, for a standard population. On average, as AV increases, consumer cost-sharing decreases. For example, for a silver-level plan, on average, a plan pays for 70% of covered services and a consumer pays for 30% of the expenses out-of-pocket.

Level	Actuarial Value
Bronze	60%
Silver	70%
Gold	80%
Platinum	90%

Source: 42 U.S.C. §18022.

Figure 3. Actuarial Value Levels.

Market Reforms

A number of ACA provisions focus on changing how health insurance plans offer coverage. Collectively, the market reforms establish federal minimum requirements regarding access to coverage, premiums, benefits, cost-sharing, and consumer protections while generally giving states the authority to enforce the reforms and the ability to expand on the reforms.[12] Some of the reforms apply to all three segments of the private insurance market (nongroup, small-group, and large-group markets). But many of the reforms focus specifically on the nongroup and small-group insurance markets, both inside and outside the exchanges.

These same market reforms apply to QHPs offered in the individual and SHOP exchanges. The reforms are intended to address perceived failures in the nongroup and small-group markets— such as limited access to coverage and higher costs of coverage—and to provide some parity with the large-group market, which may already have many of these features. The reforms generally address issues related to obtaining coverage, keeping coverage, the cost of purchasing coverage, covered benefits and services, cost-sharing limits, plan requirements, and consumer protections (some of which were discussed earlier in this report).

Other Types of Plans Offered Through Exchanges

While all health insurance plans offered through the exchanges must generally be certified QHPs, the exchanges also offer variants of QHPs and a few non-QHPs as allowed under the ACA. These QHP variants and non-QHPs are described below.

Child-Only Plans

Child-only health insurance plans are a type of QHP available in the exchanges. In order to offer child-only plans in an exchange, a health insurance plan must also offer a QHP in the exchange. The ACA requires the plan to offer the child-only exchange plan at the same level as the QHP. Only individuals under age 21 may enroll in child-only exchange plans.

Multi-State Plans

The ACA directs the Office of Personnel Management to contract with private insurance plans in each state to offer at least two comprehensive health insurance options, known as multi-state plans (MSPs). MSPs are designed to offer nationally available QHPs through the exchanges; MSPs are not available outside the exchanges. Individuals enrolled in MSP options have access to the same financial assistance for premium tax credits and cost-sharing subsidies as consumers in other plans.

Consumer Operated and Oriented Plans

The ACA includes the Consumer Operated and Oriented Plan (CO-OP) program to create nonprofit, member-run health insurance companies. The HHS Secretary is required to use funds appropriated to the CO-OP program to finance start-up and solvency loans for eligible nonprofit organizations applying to become CO-OP. The majority of the products offered by a CO-OP must be QHPs sold in the nongroup and small-group markets, including through exchanges.

Catastrophic Plans

The ACA establishes other plans that are not QHPs. One such plan is a *catastrophic plan*. A catastrophic plan offered through exchanges provides the EHB and coverage for at least three primary care visits; however, it imposes very high deductibles and does not meet the minimum requirements related to coverage generosity (i.e., actuarial value).[13] Catastrophic plans may be offered only in the individual market for (1) individuals under age 30, and (2) persons exempt from the ACA requirement to obtain health coverage (described below) because no affordable coverage is available or they have a hardship exemption.[14] Premium tax credits and cost-sharing subsidies may not be used toward catastrophic plans.

Dental-Only Plans

Dental-only plans are another type of non-QHP that may be offered in exchanges. Dental plans may be offered either as stand-alone plans or in conjunction with QHPs. Premium tax credits and cost-sharing subsidies may not be used toward dental-only plans.

EXCHANGE ENROLLMENT

Measuring exchange enrollment can be difficult. Given the exchange eligibility determination process as well as the OEPs and SEPs, data on exchange enrollment is released in stages—preeffectuated and effectuated enrollment.Pre-effectuated enrollment is the number of unique individuals who have been determined eligible to enroll in an exchange plan and have selected a plan. These individuals may or may not have submitted the first premium payment. Subsequently, effectuated enrollment is the number of unique individuals who have been determined eligible to enroll in an exchange plan, have selected a plan, and *have* submitted the first premium payment for an exchange plan.

Effectuated enrollment estimates, however, may change over time. For example, due to changes in life circumstances, an individual may un-enroll (e.g., because he or she was later offered coverage through an employer) or enroll (e.g., because he or she was eligible for a SEP) in an exchange plan.

Accordingly, exchange enrollment estimates are often reported for a particular time frame.

HHS regularly releases data on exchange enrollment. For the most current enrollment estimates, see the HHS website.[15]

Status of Exchange Implementation

This section provides a brief summary of the implementation and operation of exchanges in 2014 and to date in 2015.

2014 Coverage Year

As required by the ACA, 2014 was the first year in which health insurance coverage was available through exchanges in every state. In 2014, for the individual exchanges, 17 states had SBEs, while 34 states had FFEs. Among SHOP exchanges, 19 were SBEs and 32 were FFEs.

The OEP for 2014 coverage for all exchanges began October 1, 2013. The FFEs and some SBEs experienced difficulties related to the functionality of their websites during the OEP. In many cases the problems hindered consumers' and small businesses' ability to purchase health plans offered through exchanges. Additionally, implementation of certain features of exchanges, particularly for SHOP exchanges, was delayed for part or all of 2014. For example, small businesses using federally-facilitated SHOP exchanges were not able to purchase coverage online during any part of 2014.

One way in which HHS responded to the problems and delays was to find ways to provide access to exchange coverage to consumers and small businesses. HHS extended the OEP, identified alternative ways to enroll in coverage available through exchanges, and shortened the length of time between when an individual signed up for coverage and the date when the coverage began.

By the end of the 2014 OEP (October 1, 2013, through March 31, 2014) and a SEP (through April 19, 2014), the pre-effectuated enrollment[16] for the individual exchanges in all states and the District of Columbia was 8.0 million individuals. Among those individuals, approximately 85% received premium tax credits.[17] On October 15, 2014, the effectuated enrollment in the individual exchanges was 6.7 million individuals.[18] An estimate of how many effectuated individuals received a premium tax credit is not available. Estimates for nationwide enrollment in the SHOP exchanges in 2014 are not currently available.

2015 Coverage Year

The overall number of states with state-based and federally-facilitated individual and SHOP exchanges did not change between 2014 and 2015.

The OEP for 2015 coverage began November 1, 2014. Overall, the exchanges have had fewer operational difficulties in 2015, particularly with respect to IT infrastructure. This is the case for both state-based and federally-facilitated exchanges.

By the end of the 2015 OEP (November 15, 2014, through February 15, 2015) and a SEP (through February 22, 2015), the pre-effectuated enrollment for the individual exchanges in all states and D.C. was 11.7 million individuals. Among those individuals, approximately 87% received premium tax credits.[19] On March 31, 2015, the effectuated enrollment in the individual exchanges was 10.2 million individuals, and approximately 85% received premium tax credits.[20] As was the case in 2014, estimates for nationwide enrollment in the SHOP exchanges in 2015 are not available.

The exchanges are experiencing different challenges in 2015. For SBEs, one of those challenges is obtaining funds to sustain operations. As noted earlier in this report, exchanges are expected to be self-sustaining and can no longer obtain federal exchange grants beginning in 2015. The ACA provides that an exchange may charge an assessment or user fee to participating health plans but also allows an exchange to find other ways to generate funds to sustain its operations. Some SBEs have reported projected funding shortfalls for their exchanges and are seeking ways to secure more funding and reduce operating costs.[21]

End Notes

[1] The term *individual exchange* is used for purposes of this report. It is not defined in exchange-related statute or regulations.

[2] For detailed information about how agents and brokers can interact with exchanges, see *Resources for Agents and Brokers in the Health Insurance Marketplaces*, http://www.cms.gov/cciio/programs-and-initiatives/health-insurancemarketplaces/a-b-resources.html.

[3] State residency may be established through a variety of means, including actual or planned residence in a state, actual or planned employment in a state, and other circumstances. See 45 CFR §155.305.

[4] U.S. citizens and U.S. nationals are eligible for coverage through the exchange. "Lawfully present" immigrants are also eligible for coverage through the exchange. Examples of "lawfully present" include immigrants who have "qualified non-citizen" immigration status without a waiting period, humanitarian statuses or circumstances, valid nonimmigrant visas, and legal status conferred by other laws.

[5] For more information on employer requirements for offering employment-based coverage, see CRS Report R43981, *Affordable Care Act (ACA): Employer Shared Responsibility Determinations and Potential Penalties*.

[6] Cost-sharing is the share of costs an insured individual pays for services out-of-pocket. The term often includes deductibles, coinsurance, and co-payments. A deductible is the amount an insured individual pays before his or her health insurance plan begins to pay for services. Coinsurance is the share of costs, figured in percentage form, an insured individual pays for a health service. A co-payment is a fixed amount an insured individual pays for a health service.

[7] For more information about the annual out-of-pocket limits, see "Cost-Sharing" section of this report.

[8] This requirement applies to the small-group market operating outside of SHOP exchanges as well.

[9] It is possible for SHOP exchanges to establish minimum participation rates and minimum contribution rates. Businesses that do not comply with established rates cannot be prohibited from obtaining coverage through SHOP exchanges; rather, health insurance plans may limit the availability of coverage for any employer that does not meet an allowed minimum participation or contribution rate to an annual enrollment period—November 15 through December 15—of each year. Benefit and Payment Parameters for 2016," 80 *Federal Register* 10750-10877, February 27, 2015.

[10] The existing limits are those that are applicable to high-deductible health plans that qualify to be paired with tax-advantaged health savings accounts. For more information about these plans, see CRS Report RL32237, *Health Insurance: A Primer*.

[11] U.S. Department of Health and Human Services, "Patient Protection and Affordable Care Act: HHS Notice of

[12] Private health insurance is primarily regulated at the state level. The ACA establishes uniform requirements and additional options for all states.

[13] While catastrophic plans technically do not meet the generosity requirements for coverage, a catastrophic plan may be considered as meeting such coverage generosity requirements so long as it meets the other catastrophic plan requirements described above.

[14] Individuals who suffer a hardship with respect to the capability to obtain health insurance coverage may receive hardship exemptions. HHS has identified a number of circumstances that allow individuals to receive hardship exemptions. For more information on hardship exemptions, see CRS Report R41331, *Individual Mandate Under the ACA*.

[15] HHS, http://www.hhs.gov/healthcare/index.html.

[16] For a discussion about the differences between pre-effectuated and effectuated enrollment, see "Exchange Enrollment" section of this report.

[17] HHS, *Health Insurance Marketplace: Summary Enrollment Report for the Initial Annual Open Enrollment Period*, May 1, 2014, http:// aspe. hhs.gov/health/reports/2014/marketplaceenrollment/apr2014/ib_2014apr_enrollment.pdf.

[18] HHS, *How Many Individuals Might Have Marketplace Coverage After the 2015 Open Enrollment Period*, November 10, 2014, http://aspe.hhs.gov/ health/reports/2014/ Targets/ib_Targets.pdf.

[19] HHS, *Health Insurance Marketplace 2015 Open Enrollment Period: March Enrollment Report*, March 10, 2015, http://aspe.hhs.gov/ health/reports/ 2015/MarketPlaceEnrollment/ Mar2015/ib_2015mar_enrollment.pdf.

[20] Centers for Medicare & Medicaid Services, *March 31, 2015 Effectuated Enrollment Snapshot*, June 2, 2015, http://cms.gov Newsroom / MediaReleaseDatabase/Fact-sheets/2015-Fact-sheets-items/2015-06-02.html.

[21] Lena H. Sun and Niraj Chokshi, "Almost Half of Obamacare Exchanges Face Financial Struggles in the Future," *Washington Post*, May 1, 2015.

In: Private-Sector Health Insurance
Editor: Stephen Maxwell Mathis
ISBN: 978-1-63483-772-9

Chapter 5

HEALTH INSURANCE EXCHANGES: HEALTH INSURANCE "NAVIGATORS" AND IN-PERSON ASSISTANCE*

Suzanne M. Kirchhoff

SUMMARY

The 2010 Patient Protection and Affordable Care Act (ACA, P.L. 111-148) allows certain individuals and small businesses to buy qualified health insurance through state exchanges. The exchanges are not themselves insurers, but rather are special marketplaces where insurance firms may sell health policies that meet set, federal guidelines. As of July 2014, 14 states and the District of Columbia had secured HHS approval to create and run their own exchanges, 7 to enter into partnership exchanges, 29 to have federally facilitated exchanges, and two to have state- based SHOP/federally facilitated individual exchanges. An estimated 25 million individuals are expected to secure coverage through the exchanges by 2024.

The ACA requires exchanges to perform outreach to help consumers and small businesses make informed decisions about their insurance options,

* This is an edited, reformatted and augmented version of a Congressional Research Service publication R43243, prepared for Members and Committees of Congress dated August 13, 2014.

including the operation of "navigator" programs. Navigators carry out public education activities; provide information to prospective enrollees about insurance options and federal assistance; and examine enrollees' eligibility for other federal or state health care programs, such as Medicaid. Navigators may assist consumers in comparing insurance plans, but may not determine their eligibility for subsidies or enroll them in plans—functions that are left to the exchanges. A variety of organizations may become navigators, including labor unions, trade associations, chambers of commerce, and other entities. Navigators may not be health insurers or take compensation from insurers for selling health policies. Navigators must have 20 hours of training on consumer privacy, exchange-based insurance offerings, and other issues. HHS has provided about $60 million in yearly grants for navigators at federally financed and state partnership exchanges. In addition, HHS has determined that state-based exchanges may use ACA exchange establishment funds to create parallel, in- person, non-navigator assistance programs that perform the same function as navigators. Exchanges must also certify "certified application counselors" to help with outreach and enrollment, though no new ACA funds are available for such programs.

Consumers and small businesses may continue to use insurance brokers and agents, including web-based brokers, to compare and buy coverage, both on and off the exchanges. Brokers and agents are licensed by the states, and are generally paid on a commission basis by insurance companies. While brokers and agents may choose to become navigators, they may not accept compensation from health insurance companies in that role. Consumers may also purchase policies directly from health insurers. Outside non-profit groups and businesses, such as insurers, operate their own separate efforts to educate consumers about the ACA and the process of applying for qualified health plans (QHP) and other programs.

Some lawmakers, agents, and brokers have raised questions about the navigator and other assistance programs. Issues include whether navigators have sufficient training and whether HHS regulations provide sufficiently stringent consumer and privacy safeguards. A number of states have passed legislation to further regulate navigators, including requiring navigators to be licensed and to be liable for financial losses due to their advice. HHS has determined that the ACA gives states authority to set additional standards, so long as they do not prevent implementation of Title I of the law, which includes the exchanges and navigator program. This report describes exchange outreach programs, the role of brokers, agents, and insurers, and issues regarding consumer outreach assistance.

INTRODUCTION

The 2010 Patient Protection and Affordable Care Act (ACA, P.L. 111-148 as amended) mandated the creation of state health care exchanges for the sale of insurance policies, including certain individual and small-group policies.[1] Under the ACA, a state may set up its own exchange or create an exchange in partnership with the federal government. If a state chooses not to form an exchange, or cannot meet ACA requirements, the Department of Health and Human Services (HHS) will run its exchange. (See text box below, "Glossary of ACA Terms.")

As of July 2014, 14 states and the District of Columbia had secured HHS approval to create their own exchanges, 7 to enter into partnership exchanges, 29 to have federally facilitated exchanges, and 2 to have state-based SHOP/federally facilitated individual exchanges. The exchanges began offering insurance on October 1, 2013. The insurance policies, and the exchanges, were fully operational on January 1, 2014.[2]

An exchange is not an insurer, but is rather a type of marketplace where private insurance companies may sell qualified health plans (QHP) that meet certain federal standards.[3] Consumers, businesses, and issuers are not required to use the exchanges to purchase insurance. However, individuals must buy exchange-based coverage to qualify for federal premium tax credits and cost-sharing subsidies.[4] Small businesses that apply for coverage through the exchanges may be eligible for small business tax credits.[5] Consumers may apply for coverage over the phone, online, via mail, or in person in some areas.

The Congressional Budget Office (CBO) projects that 25 million individuals will be enrolled in health insurance through the exchanges in 2024.[6] New enrollees are expected to be poorer, more racially and ethnically diverse, less educated, and less familiar with insurance than those who currently have health insurance coverage.[7] To help these consumers negotiate the enrollment process, the ACA requires exchanges to perform education and outreach functions. Exchanges may use a variety of techniques to reach out to the public including mailings, brochures, social media, corporate partnerships, health fairs, and other public events.

Glossary of ACA Terms

State-Based Exchange—As exchange set up and run by a state, following ACA guidelines. Can be designed as a non- profit or governmental entity. Under a state-based exchange, HHS may carry out some functions, such as reinsurance, risk adjustment, and determining eligibility for premium subsidies, and tax credits.

Federally Facilitated Exchange—If a state chooses not to operate its own exchange, or does not have approval to operate its own exchange, the Secretary of HHS is required to establish a federally facilitated exchange in the state. Either states or the federal government may perform some exchange functions such as reinsurance and determining eligibility for federal health care programs.

State Partnership Exchange—A state may enter into a "partnership" with a federally facilitated exchange, combining state-designed and -operated functions with federally designed and operated functions. Partnership exchanges are considered a subset of federally facilitated exchanges, indicating that HHS has authority over partnerships in a federally facilitated exchange. Under this arrangement, states administer and operate plan management and/or consumer assistance activities.

SHOP—Small Business Health Options Program that assists small businesses in enrolling employees in qualified health plans offered in the small-employer market. A SHOP may be part of a larger exchange or a stand-alone exchange run by the state or federal government. The SHOP exchange is responsible for collecting and verifying information from employers and employees, determining eligibility, and facilitating enrollment.

Individual Exchange—Part of a larger exchange or a stand-alone exchange where individuals may shop for qualified health plans, apply for premium subsidies, and enroll in individual health plans. Individuals will also receive assistance in determining whether they qualify for Medicaid or other government programs. May be part of a larger federal or state exchange, or a stand-alone exchange.

State-based SHOP/federally facilitated Individual Exchange—Hybrid system where a state establishes and administers a SHOP exchange and the federal government sets up and runs the individual exchange for the state.

CONSUMER ASSISTANCE PROGRAMS

Under the ACA and implementing regulations issued by the HHS Centers for Medicare & Medicaid Services (CMS), consumer assistance[8] outreach programs include the following:

- Mandatory navigator programs[9] designed to provide "fair and impartial" information about exchange-based insurance plans, as well as the availability of federal assistance to help defray the cost of insurance and other health programs.
- Non-navigator or "in-person assistance" programs at state-run exchanges and state partnership exchanges.[10] The non-navigators perform generally the same functions as navigators,[11] or complement the role of navigators by reaching out to underserved populations, but have a separate source of federal funding via exchange establishment grants. Non-navigators are optional at state exchanges, and mandatory at certain partnership exchanges.
- Certified application counselors to help individuals apply for QHP enrollment and possible subsidies.[12] Exchanges may designate various organizations or individuals as application counselors or allow outside organizations to certify the counselors. Counselors are mandatory, but their duties are more limited than those of navigators and non-navigators. No new ACA funds were provided for the counselors, though they may be funded through existing state, local, or federal programs.

In addition, consumers and businesses may use insurance brokers and agents, including web- based brokers (where allowed by states), to purchase QHPs.[13] Brokers and agents, licensed by states, are generally paid a commission by insurance companies for selling their policies. Brokers and agents may apply to serve as navigators, but may not accept direct or indirect compensation from health or stop-loss insurers in this role.

Under CMS rules, consumers may also go directly to insurance companies to obtain information about QHPs and other insurance options, and to sign up for such plans.[14]

Some lawmakers, as well as brokers and agents, have questioned whether CMS regulations impose sufficient training and consumer safeguards for the navigator, non-navigator, and consumer assistance programs. A number of states have passed legislation to require navigators to have additional training and licensing, or to undergo background checks.[15] The ACA gives states flexibility to certify or license navigators, but state actions may not prevent the implementation of Title I of the ACA, which authorizes the exchanges. CMS has interpreted the law to mean that states may not require all navigators, for example, to be licensed as insurance agents or brokers.[16] (See "State and Exchange Licensing and Certification.") This report outlines federal and state oversight of navigators, the role of brokers and agents, and previous education and outreach efforts for federal health care programs.

Navigator Program

The navigator program is described in Section 1311(i) of the ACA. Exchanges are required to have navigators who will perform duties that include

- conducting public education activities to raise awareness of the availability of QHPs;
- distributing fair and impartial information concerning enrollment in QHPs, and the availability of premium tax credits and cost-sharing assistance;
- facilitating enrollment in QHPs;
- referring any enrollee with a grievance, complaint, or question regarding a health plan to an applicable office of health insurance consumer assistance, a health insurance ombudsman, or any other appropriate state agency or agencies; and
- providing information that is culturally and linguistically appropriate to the population being served by the exchange.

The ACA directed the Secretary of HHS (Secretary) to establish standards for the navigator program, in collaboration with states. The Secretary is to ensure that navigators are qualified and licensed, if appropriate, and to set standards to avoid conflicts of interest in the program.

CMS regulations to implement the ACA specify that navigators may offer consumers assistance in comparing and analyzing insurance options, but may not tell applicants which health plan to select. In addition, exchanges, rather than navigators, formally determine whether an applicant is eligible for tax credits and other assistance to defray the cost of health coverage. Exchanges also formally enroll applicants into QHPs, with some exceptions.[17]

Eligibility to Become a Navigator

The ACA includes a list of organizations and individuals eligible to become navigators, including trade, industry, and professional associations; commercial fishing industry organizations; ranching and farming organizations; community and consumer-focused non-profit groups; chambers of commerce; unions; small business development centers; and licensed insurance agents and brokers.[18] The list is illustrative rather than definitive, and other organizations may apply for navigator status. At least one navigator for each exchange must be from a community, non-profit organization.[19]

Under the ACA, a navigator may not be a health insurer or receive direct or indirect consideration from a health insurer in connection with enrolling individuals or employees in QHPs or non- QHPs.[20] CMS regulations further bar individuals or organizations from serving as navigators if they are issuers of stop loss insurance and their subsidiaries; associations that include members of or that lobby for the insurance industry; or entities that receive direct or indirect consideration from a health insurance or stop loss insurance issuer in connection with enrolling individuals or workers in a QHP or non-QHP.[21] Stop loss insurance is a type of insurance that takes effect after a company or issuer has paid out a certain level of health care claims. Entities that self-insure (finance their own health insurance plans) often use stop-loss coverage to limit their expenses.[22]

Insurance brokers and agents may apply to become navigators, but under CMS rules they may not accept compensation from health or stop loss insurers in this role. (See "Brokers and Agents.") However, a health care provider is not barred from becoming a navigator solely because it receives payment from a health insurance issuer for providing services.[23]

In instances when a state operates a SHOP exchange, but that state's individual exchange is run by the federal government, CMS will allow two separate navigator programs. Such states will have a federal navigator program for the individual exchange, and a state navigator program for the SHOP. SHOP navigators could fulfill their obligation to facilitate enrollment, and refer consumers with complaints or questions to applicable government offices, by referring small businesses to agents and brokers for this type of assistance, so long as applicable state law permits agents and brokers to carry out these functions.[24]

Navigators must maintain a physical presence in their exchange service area. Navigators working for federally facilitated exchanges are not required to have their principal place of business in the exchange service area, however.[25]

Navigator Application Process

CMS in April 2013 released its initial cooperative agreement funding application[26] for individuals and organizations seeking to become navigators at federally facilitated and partnership exchanges. On August 15, 2013, CMS awarded $67 million in 12-month grants to 105 navigator organizations.[27] The grants expire in August 2014. (See "Navigator and Non-navigator Funding.") In June 2014, CMS released a funding application for $60 million in new 12-month grants for navigators in federally facilitated and state partnership exchanges. The grants are to be awarded, and take effect, in September 2014.[28]

Organizations and individuals that apply for the navigator program are required to submit certain information to CMS, including[29]

- a plan for carrying out outreach and education activities specified in the ACA and in CMS regulations;
- a description of existing relationships with employers and employees, consumers (including uninsured and underinsured consumers), or self-employed individuals likely to be eligible to enroll in a qualified health plan; or a description of how such relationships could be readily established;
- a statement attesting that the applicant is not ineligible for the program due to a financial or other relationship with health insurers;
- a plan to perform the statutory and regulatory duties of a navigator for the entire length of the agreement;
- an attestation that staff and volunteers will remain free of conflicts of interest while acting as a navigator;
- a plan to ensure that staff and volunteers complete all required training; and
- a plan to comply with data privacy and security standards.

Navigator applications are evaluated on criteria that include the scope of their planned activities; their planned budget; their background and experience; and their expertise in health issues, outreach, and working with underserved and vulnerable populations. Navigators must provide weekly, monthly, quarterly and final reports on their work, and comply with CMS evaluations. While navigator organizations are not required to perform background checks on their staff, navigator applications that do have a plan for background checks may receive a higher score on their grant application.[30]

Non-Navigator/Assister Programs

CMS allows, but does not require, state-based exchanges to establish non-navigator or assister programs that perform the same basic functions as navigators.[31] States that have entered into consumer partnership exchanges[32] are required as a condition of the partnership to create non- navigator programs, in addition to their navigator programs. State-based exchanges, and states in consumer partnership exchanges, may use ACA Section 1311 exchange establishment grants for non-navigator programs during their first year of operation.[33] The ACA prohibits exchanges from using Section 1311 exchange establishment grants for regular navigator programs, with some limited exceptions.

Table 1. Types of Consumer Assistance Available at Exchanges

Location		Funding
Navigators	All exchanges.	Funded through state and federal grant programs.
In-Person Assisters/Non-Navigators	Optional for state-based exchange, Mandatory for consumer partnership exchange.	Funded through separate ACA grants or by states.
Certified Application Counselors	All exchanges.	May be funded through existing state, federal, and other programs.
Agents and Brokers	All exchanges, if allowed by states.	Compensated by insurers.

Source: Centers for Medicare & Medicaid Services.

Notes: Agents and brokers may serve as navigators if they agree not to take any compensation from health insurers for insurance sales and also meet other standards.

CMS created the non-navigator program to address the possibility that some exchanges might not have sufficient money for education and outreach during their early months of operation. State- based exchanges can use non-navigators to fill in any gaps in their navigator programs, and provide a full range of services during their first year.[34] Possible funding for following years is not clear. The ACA requires that each exchange be self-sustaining, beginning January 1, 2015. The ACA provides that an exchange may charge an assessment or user fee to participating issuers, but also allows an exchange to find other ways to generate funds to sustain its operations, which include continuing education and outreach activities.[35]

Like navigators, non-navigators may not be issuers of health insurance and their subsidiaries, including stop-loss insurance; associations that include members of or that lobby for the insurance industry; or entities that receive direct or indirect consideration from a health insurance or stop-loss insurance issuer in connection with enrolling individuals or workers in a QHP or non-QHP. Non-navigator programs at consumer partnership exchanges, and state-based exchanges funded through ACA exchange grants, are subject to the same training and conflict-of-interest restrictions as navigators.[36] State-based exchanges that create non-navigator programs with their own money, rather than with exchange establishment funds, are encouraged, but not required, to use CMS navigator standards. Non-navigators in federally funded exchanges and state exchanges must maintain a physical presence in the exchange areas. Non-navigators in federally funded exchanges do not have to have their principal place of business in the exchange area.[37]

State-run exchanges have some flexibility in defining the roles of in-person assistance or non- navigator personnel and determining how their duties mesh with those of the navigators. For example, states can require non-navigators to target different demographic groups or perform different functions than navigators.[38]

Certified Application Counselors

CMS regulations require state exchanges to have certified application counselor programs to help facilitate enrollment in QHPs.[39] There is no new federal funding for the counselors, though state- based exchanges may use Section 1311 establishment funds for counselor training.[40] Exchanges are not prohibited from using existing private, state, or federal programs to fund the counselors.

Federally facilitated exchanges may designate organizations to certify their staff or volunteers to perform as certified application counselors. Exchanges must focus on organizations that already have systems in place for protecting personally sensitive data, such as state Medicaid and CHIP agencies, hospitals and other health care providers, or social service agencies.[41] State-based marketplaces may designate outside organizations to certify staff and volunteers as application counselors, or may directly certify application counselors.[42]

Like navigators and non-navigators, certified application counselors are to provide information regarding the full range of QHPs offered at an exchange and health insurance affordability programs. The counselors must work "in the best interest" of enrollees when helping individuals and employees apply for QHPs and other coverage.[43] Counselors must go through exchange- approved training and comply with data security and privacy standards and applicable state and federal laws.[44] They may work through an exchange or navigators and non-navigators to provide appropriate services to people with disabilities or to address complaints, grievances, and other questions.[45] Certified application counselors must be recertified on at least an annual basis and must meet any licensing, certification, or other standards set by a state or exchange, so long as the standards do not prevent the implementation of the ACA.[46]

Certified application counselors may not receive consideration directly or indirectly from any health insurance issuer or issuer of stop-loss insurance in connection with the enrollment of any individual in a QHP or a non-QHP.[47] Health providers or other entities may not be disqualified from becoming certified application counselors solely because they receive payment from a health insurer for providing health care services.[48] Certified application counselors do not have to maintain a physical place of business in the exchange area, and counselors working for a federally funded exchange do not have to have their principal place of business in the exchange area.[49]

Federally Qualified Health Centers

CMS in 2013 provided $150 million in grants to more than 1,100 community health centers, which may serve as application counselors, to help enroll consumers in QHPs.[50] CMS provided an additional $58 million to the health centers in December 2013 to help during final enrollment.[51]

Conflict-of-Interest Rules

Navigators and non-navigators funded through Section 1311 exchange establishment funding must attest that they are eligible entities and submit a written plan to remain free of conflicts while serving in these roles.[52]

CMS regulations (45 C.F.R. 155.215) state that certain business arrangements or relationships are not necessarily a bar to serving as a navigator or a non-navigator, so long as they do not prevent an entity from providing information and services in a fair, accurate, and impartial manner. To mitigate possible conflicts of interest, CMS requires covered navigators and non-navigators to reveal certain information regarding possible conflicts of interest to exchanges and consumers.

Additional information to be disclosed[53] includes background about

- any lines of insurance, other than health care or stop loss coverage, that a navigator intends to sell while serving as a navigator;
- any existing and former employment relationship during the past five years with an issuer of health or stop-loss insurance or a subsidiary;
- any existing employment relationship between any issuer of health care or stop loss insurance and an individual's spouse or domestic partner; and
- any existing or anticipated financial, business, or contractual relationships with one or more issuers of health or stop-loss insurance or their subsidiaries.

If an entity or organization is awarded a navigator or non-navigator grant, conflict-of-interest rules apply to its entire staff. Certified application counselors must disclose potential conflicts of interest either to an exchange or an exchange-designated organization.[54]

Exchange Standards

In May 2014 CMS issued final rules designed to further protect enrollees and prevent possible abuse in outreach and enrollment activities. The rules require navigators, non-navigators, and certified application counselors to ensure that applicants are informed of the functions and responsibilities of navigators and other assistance personnel. In addition, they must obtain authorization from a consumer prior to obtaining access to the consumer's personally identifiable information and maintain a record of the authorization.[55] A consumer may revoke the authorization at any time.[56]

In addition, the final rules state that navigators, non-navigators and certified application counselors

- May not be compensated by their organizations on a per-application, per- individual assistance, or per-enrollment basis. The provision, which takes effect on November 15, 2014, applies to federally funded exchanges.[57]
- May not charge any applicant or enrollee, or request or receive any form of remuneration from or on behalf of an individual applicant or enrollee, for assistance related to assister duties.[58]
- May not provide gifts, gift cards, or cash of more than nominal value ($15) or items of any value that market or promote products or services of a third party.[59] (Gifts, gift cards, or cash that exceed nominal value may be used to reimburse applicants for legitimate expenses incurred while seeking assistance through an exchange, such as postage or travel expenses.)[60]
- May not solicit consumers for application or enrollment assistance by going door-to-door or through other direct contact such as a phone call, unless the consumer initiates contact or has a preexisting relationship with the assister organization and other applicable state and federal laws are complied with.[61] Outreach and education activities may be conducted by going door-to-door or through other unsolicited contact, including phone calls.
- May not use automatic telephone dialing systems or prerecorded voice messages to initiate contact with a potential enrollee unless there is a preexisting relationship with the consumer and other applicable laws are complied with.

CMS rules also allow consumers to change plans if assisters make an error in their application. (See "Special Enrollment Period.")

Training and Certification

CMS regulations include training standards[63] for federally facilitated exchanges, including partnership exchanges, and for non-navigators at state-run exchanges funded through Section 1311 grants. The CMS training standards may also be used by state exchanges for their navigator programs and for any non-navigator programs funded outside of Section 1311 grants. State exchanges may also develop their own training, with approval by HHS.[64]

SPECIAL ENROLLMENT PERIOD

Under CMS regulations, exchanges must allow qualified individuals and enrollees to enroll in or change from one QHP to another in certain instances, such as gaining a dependent through birth or marriage or becoming a U.S. citizen.[62] In addition, an individual may change plans when:

A qualified individual's, or his or her dependent's, enrollment or non-enrollment in a QHP is unintentional, inadvertent, or erroneous and is the result of the error, misrepresentation, or inaction of an officer, employee, or agent of the Exchange or HHS, or its instrumentalities as evaluated and determined by the Exchange. In such cases, the Exchange may take such action as may be necessary to correct or eliminate the effects of such error, misrepresentation, or inaction.

Navigator and Non-navigator Training

To be certified by an exchange, navigator and non-navigator personnel at federally facilitated exchanges, including partnership exchanges, and all federally funded non-navigators at state- based exchanges, must

- Complete 20 hours of HHS-approved training and receive a passing score on HHS-approved exams. Annual certification or recertification is required. [65]
- Be prepared to serve both the individual and SHOP exchanges and to provide services that meet the language and cultural needs of various populations, and of disabled individuals.

CMS originally called for up to 30 hours of training, but reduced the required training to 20 hours.[66] State-run exchanges may have much more extensive training.[67]

CMS rules require that navigators and covered non-navigators undergo training that includes eligibility and enrollment rules and processes; the full range of QHPs offered at an exchange; the range of insurance options including Medicaid and CHIP and other public programs; eligibility requirements for government assistance; the tax implications of enrollment decisions; privacy and security requirements; how to appeal an enrollment decision; outreach methods; and how to work effectively with people with disabilities or limited language skills. Privacy training must include processes for safeguarding health information, income and tax information, and Social Security numbers. The CMS August 2013 *Health Insurance Marketplace Navigator Standard Operating Procedures Manual* is a guide for navigators in helping consumers.[68]

The regulations also require that navigators must develop, maintain, and regularly update a body of general knowledge about the racial, ethnic, and cultural groups in their service areas, including the primary language spoken. Navigators and non-navigators must provide information in a consumer's preferred language at no cost to the consumer, as well as auxiliary aids and services for the disabled, at no cost where necessary.[69] Navigators and non-navigators are required to recruit and promote a staff that is representative of the demographic characteristics of their service area, including the languages spoken. Navigators and non-navigators must also provide appropriate materials and assistance to individuals with disabilities.

Certified Application Counselor Training

Certified application counselors must complete and achieve a passing score on a certification exam. Training materials are more limited than for the navigator program,[70] because the counselor program is more limited. For example, counselors do not have to receive training regarding certain federal health programs since they will not be directly referring potential enrollees to such programs. Counselors could also refer individuals with disabilities to navigator or non-navigator programs or to an exchange call center to ensure they receive appropriate services.

Privacy Protections

CMS regulations to implement the ACA include rules and procedures designed to protect enrollee privacy (45 C.F.R. 155.260). (See the **Appendix**.) The privacy and information requirements, which are in addition to other applicable state and federal laws, generally limit the collection, use, retention, and disclosure of personally identifiable information such as Social Security numbers. CMS regulations require exchanges to include these security and privacy requirements in any contract with non-exchange entities such as navigators, brokers, and agents that

- gain access to personally identifiable information submitted to an exchange; or
- collect, use, or disclose personally identifiable information gathered directly from applicants, qualified individuals, or enrollees while that individual or entity is performing the functions outlined in the agreement with the exchange.[71]

CMS regulations also require that navigators and non-navigators receive training in privacy standards and procedures, as part of their overall training. Personnel who willingly violate exchange privacy and security policies are subject to a fine of up to $25,000 per disclosure. States may set additional eligibility criteria and background checks for navigators and non-navigators, so long as they do not prevent the application of Title I of the Affordable Care Act.

CMS has taken other actions in the case of certified application counselors.[72] Federally facilitated exchanges will only designate outside organizations that (1) have processes in place to screen their staff members and volunteers who are certified application counselors to ensure that they protect personally identifiable information, (2) engage in services that position them to help those they serve with health coverage issues, and (3) have experience providing social services to the community. The organizations must submit an application to an exchange and agree to comply with applicable rules and statutes. Exchanges can withdraw from the arrangements if outside organizations and their staff do not meet agreed terms or violate privacy standards, for example.

Brokers and agents are to comply with exchange privacy and security standards through agreements with federally facilitated exchanges. The agreements will spell out how agents and brokers may use personally identifiable information and their duties to protect such data and train staff in use of the information. They will also prohibit the use of such data for any purpose other than the specific functions in the agreement, related to exchange enrollment.[73]

CMS will monitor federally facilitated exchanges, as well as non-exchange entities associated with the exchange, for compliance with privacy and security standards established by the exchange. In addition, the HHS will oversee and monitor state exchanges, while the state exchanges will oversee non-exchange entities required to comply with the privacy and security standards set out by a state exchange. HHS oversight may include audits, investigations, inspections, and other activities.[74]

Federally facilitated exchanges, non-exchange entities associated with federal exchanges, and state-based exchanges will be required to report any privacy or security incident or breach to HHS.[75] Non-exchange entities associated with state exchanges will be required to report incidents and breaches to a state exchange.

State and Exchange Licensing and Certification

The ACA gives states and exchanges authority to impose additional licensing, certification, or other standards for navigators.[76] The ACA also contains a provision clarifying that state laws that do not prevent implementation of Title I of the ACA (which creates the exchanges and the navigator program) are not preempted by the ACA.[77]

CMS regulations interpret the ACA to mean that licensing, certification, and other state and exchange standards apply so long as they do not prevent the application of ACA Title I.[78] Along those lines, CMS has determined that states and exchanges are prohibited from imposing any requirement that would, in effect, require all navigators to be licensed agents or brokers.[79]

ACA regulations define an agent or broker as ''a person or entity licensed by the State as an agent, broker, or insurance producer.''[80] According to CMS, if states required that every navigator go through a specific licensing process to become an agent or broker, then agents and brokers would be the only types of navigators allowed to operate at the exchanges. That, in turn, would violate a provision of ACA rules[81] mandating that each exchange have at least two different types of navigators, including one community or consumer-focused non-profit group. The list of organizations and individuals eligible to become navigators includes chambers of commerce, unions, and health workers. (See "Eligibility to Become a Navigator.")

In May 2014, CMS issued final rules that provide additional guidance regarding potential state standards that would prevent the application of ACA Title 1.[82] State standards that would prevent application of Title 1 include, but are not limited to

- requirements that navigators and non-navigators refer consumers to other entities not required to provide fair, accurate, and impartial information;

- requirements that would prevent navigators and non-navigators from providing services to all persons to whom they are required to provide assistance;[83]
- requirements that would prevent navigators and non-navigators from providing advice regarding substantive benefits or comparative benefits of different health plans; and
- imposing standards that would, as applied or as implemented in a state, prevent the application of federal requirements applicable to navigator and non- navigators entities or individuals or applicable to the exchange's implementation of the navigator and non-navigator program.

Navigator and Non-navigator Funding

Federally facilitated exchanges and partnership exchanges use federal Prevention and Public Health Fund (PPHF) dollars for grants to navigators. CMS on August 15, 2013, awarded $67 million in 12-month grants to 105 organizations at federally facilitated and partnership exchanges. The grantees began assisting with enrollment in October 2013.[84] (See **Table 2.**)

Table 2. 2013 Federal Navigator Grants to Top 10 States with Highest Uninsured

Grants are for programs at federally facilitated and partnership exchanges. (In millions of dollars)

State	Number of Uninsured Under Age 65	Initial Navigator Funding Allocation
Texas	4,888,650	$10.8
Florida	3,509,164	$7.8
Georgia	1,698,883	$3.8
Illinois	1,403,613	$3.1
Ohio	1,354,868	$3.0
North Carolina	1,346,601	$3.0
Pennsylvania	1,242,351	$2.7
Michigan	1,145,493	$2.5
Arizona	947,880	$2.1
Indiana	909,633	$2.0
New Jersey	901,290	$2.0

Source: CMS, Cooperative Agreement to Support Navigators in Federally-facilitated and State Partnership Exchanges. Grants are funded for a 12-month period from the date of the award.

CMS allocated the funding for each state based on the number of uninsured residents in the state under the age of 65 as a share of the overall number of uninsured in states with a federally facilitated or partnership exchange. The amount of funding awarded to each navigator via the application process was based on the breadth of its proposed educational and outreach activities and the size of the population to be served. Each navigator applicant was eligible for one non- renewable, one-year cooperative agreement award, though HHS may end funding early in certain cases.[85] Grantees included food banks, county commissioners, hospitals and health systems, universities, legal aid societies, Planned Parenthood chapters, a health plan for uninsured fishermen, and American Indian health services.

CMS has announced a second round of navigator grants, for the 12-month period beginning in September 2014. Each participating state will be eligible for at least $600,000 in navigator funding.[86]

Section 1311 of the ACA provides indefinite (i.e., unspecified) amounts of money for planning and establishment grants for exchanges. For each fiscal year, the Secretary is to determine the total to be made available to each state for exchange grants. However, no grant may be awarded after January 1, 2015.[87] ACA Section 1311 (i)(6) prohibits exchanges from using Section 1311 establishment funds to fund navigator grants. CMS regulations allow state-based exchanges and consumer partnership exchanges to use Section 1311 exchange grants to fund non-navigator assistance programs during their initial year of operation.[88] Section 1311 funds may also be used to cover an exchange's cost of administering the navigator program, including training, grants management, and oversight.[89]

State-based exchanges appear to have spent more for outreach than have federally facilitated exchanges. A study of select exchanges by The Urban Institute found that state exchanges spent an average of $30.66 in outreach per beneficiary, compared to $11.49 at federally facilitated and partnership exchanges.[90] The study also found that states operating their own exchanges tended to have more stringent training requirements. Likewise, a Kaiser Family Foundation survey found that states with partnership or state-run exchanges had about twice as many assisters per 10,000 uninsured consumers as states with federally facilitated exchanges.[91]

Brokers and Agents

U.S. health insurance agents and brokers, collectively called "producers," are a contact point between insurance companies and applicants, helping individuals and businesses choose suitable policies.[92] According to the Bureau of Labor Statistics (BLS), producers selling all types of insurance, including health policies, held about 443,400 jobs in 2012 and had median annual wages of $48,150.[93] Insurance producers are a major segment of the U.S. financial services industry, offering annuity products, comprehensive financial planning services, such as retirement and estate planning, and business pension planning.[94]

Though insurance producers work with consumers, they are paid by insurance companies. An agent may be a so-called captive agent who works for one insurance firm, or an independent agent who sells products from a variety of insurers. Independent agents may be paid via commission, while those working for an agency or insurer may receive a salary, often plus commission or bonus. An insurance broker generally represents a wider array of insurance products than an agent, and assumes a greater role in assessing the potential risk profile and insurance requirements of a client, including overall insurance needs and appropriate policies.

A web-based insurance broker may offer products from a variety of insurers on a central website. Potential clients enter basic information into the site, such as zip code and family size, and are then presented with an array of possible insurance plans. Shoppers can search for plans in different ways such as company name, average monthly cost, premiums, and other variables.

Licensing

With the exception of government-sponsored insurance programs (e.g., Medicare Advantage), agent and broker activity usually is regulated by the states,[95] which prohibit unfair sales practices and require producers to meet certain standards to become licensed.

The ACA includes several provisions that affect brokers and agents. In addition to the navigator/non-navigator program, the ACA's Medical Loss Ratio (MLR) provisions require certain large group health plans to spend at least 85% of revenues on benefits to enrollees, rather than administration or profits, while small group and individual plans must meet an 80% MLR requirement. Under CMS regulations, commissions and fees paid to brokers and agents are counted as insurance company administrative costs. Producers say that some insurance companies have reduced their commissions in an effort to contain administrative costs and meet the MLR requirements.[96]

Exchange Requirements

Agents and brokers play a role in selling QHPs to both individuals and small businesses. CMS regulations[97] were designed to allow exchanges to "leverage the market presence of agents and brokers ... to draw consumers to the Exchange and to QHPs." Exchanges may allow agents and brokers to help individuals enroll directly through an exchange website, or through outside issuer web sites, so long as they meet certain exchange standards and safeguards. Brokers or agents that discover that a potential client is qualified for federal health programs, such as Medicaid or CHIP, are expected to direct them to the appropriate public agency for assistance.[98]

Federally Facilitated and Partnership Exchanges

CMS regulations set out processes for licensed agents, brokers, and web-based brokers to help consumers and employers enroll in QHPs through federally facilitated exchanges, as well as to continue to sell other, off-exchange insurance options. Federally facilitated and partnership exchanges do not pay commissions to brokers, nor do they place a cap on agent and broker commissions for selling QHPs. CMS rules do, however, require insurance companies to pay similar broker compensation for QHPs offered through such exchanges, as for similar health plans offered outside such exchanges.[99]

In states with federally facilitated or partnership exchanges, CMS requires[100] agents and brokers to register by providing proof of identity, completing an exchange-specific training course, and agreeing to comply with federal and state laws and regulations, including those regarding privacy and security.

After producers have completed the required steps and are certified by an exchange they receive an exchange user ID, which they can use, along with their national producer number, to make transactions and receive compensation from insurers.

Brokers and agents at federally facilitated and partnership exchanges can assist consumers either

- through an issuer-based pathway, using an insurer's website, or
- through an exchange pathway, with the agent or broker helping the consumer on an exchange website.

For federally facilitated SHOP exchanges, agents and brokers will use the exchange website to carry out employer and employee applications.[101]

Issuer-Based Enrollment

Since the fall of 2013, insurance agents have been allowed to assist individuals seeking QHPs by directly using insurance/issuer websites. Insurers are to assign agents and brokers to sell their products, are to check the agent or broker's license status, and are to ensure that the agent or broker is certified by an exchange.

An agent starts the signup process by logging on to an insurer's website (this is applicable in situations where the issuer has satisfied exchange requirements and has direct enrollment ability). Once a consumer is ready to apply for a QHP, the issuer website will redirect the producer and the consumer to the exchange website to complete the eligibility application. As part of the process, agents and brokers are expected to disclose to the consumer that they are providing information about QHPs for which they have a business relationship, and to tell the potential enrollee that he or she may look at other QHP options on the exchange. After the consumer is verified as eligible to buy a QHP, the exchange will redirect the producer and client back to the insurer's website to compare plans and make a selection.

Exchange Website

Agents and brokers may assist consumers and qualified small employers and their employees directly on an exchange website. Agents and brokers may help consumers create exchange accounts, but the consumer (or an authorized representative) must create his or her own secure password and user name and should not share that information with third parties, including producers. When an agent uses an exchange website, all QHPs are to be displayed.

State-Based Exchanges

State-based exchanges will continue to license and regulate agents and brokers, including those who sell QHPs through the exchange. States may require continuing education or exchange-based training for producers, including state-specific training. States may implement additional requirements, such as mandating that producers provide information to consumers about all available QHPs, not just those for which they receive a commission. State-based exchanges may allow brokers and agents to be directly compensated through an exchange or through issuer-based commissions, and may allow agents and brokers to help enroll an individual in a QHP in a "manner than constitutes enrollment through the exchange."

Web-Based Brokerages

Federally facilitated and partnership exchanges are to work with web-based brokers, to the extent allowed by a state (the main entity licensing and regulating agents and brokers). While state- based marketplaces have latitude to set conditions for web-based brokers, CMS regulations require that the exchanges must perform enrollee eligibility determinations for individuals who sign up for QHPs. In addition, the state-based exchanges must transmit enrollment information to QHP issuers for all individuals enrolling through the marketplace.

CMS regulations impose additional marketing restrictions on web-based brokers to ensure, in part, that consumers do not mistake their websites for official exchange websites.[102] Web-based brokers must display available information on QHPs offered through an exchange, and provide consumers with the ability to view all exchange QHPs. Web brokers may not provide financial incentives, such as rebates or giveaways, and must allow consumers to withdraw from the application process and use the exchange website at any time.[103]

CMS will require web-based brokers to display a disclaimer including the fact that their website might not contain all QHP information available on the exchange website. Web brokers selling products offered on federally facilitated exchanges will have to use an HHS-approved disclaimer indicating that the website is not a federally facilitated exchange website, that their website might not contain all QHP information available on the exchange website, and that the broker is subject to exchange marketing and privacy regulations. Brokers must also provide links to the appropriate exchange.[104] CMS is currently developing guidance regarding display of such disclaimers.

Direct Enrollment through Insurers

CMS anticipates some consumers may contact insurance companies directly to enroll in QHPs. In such cases, exchanges would have the option of allowing insurers to enroll the consumers into QHPs in a manner that is considered to be enrollment through an exchange. Under CMS rules, in order for issuer enrollment to be considered as enrollment through an exchange, the insurer's website must provide applicants the option of looking at all QHPs offered by the insurer, distinguish between QHPs for which the consumer is eligible and other health plans that the insurer may offer, and make clear that the tax credits and subsidies apply only to QHPs through an exchange. The insurer must use an HHS-approved disclaimer to let consumers know of other QHPs through the exchange, as well as provide a weblink to the exchange.[105] In addition, the insurer must charge the enrollee the same premium that is charged for the QHP on an exchange, after accounting for any federal subsidy.

If permitted by an exchange, and to the extent permitted by state law, an insurer may allow its issuer application assisters[106] to help consumers apply for an eligibility determination through an exchange; apply for tax credits and other cost-sharing; and help select a QHP offered by the issuer. There must be an agreement between the insurer and the exchange under which the issuer application assisters (1) are trained in QHP options, insurance affordability programs, eligibility, and benefit rules and regulations; (2) comply with exchange privacy and security standards; and (3) comply with state laws regarding the sale, solicitation, and negotiation of health insurance products, including laws related to agent, broker, and producer licensing; confidentiality; and conflicts of interest.[107]

Previous Insurance Education and Outreach Efforts

HHS has carried out previous, major health insurance education and enrollment efforts, including enrollment efforts under the Medicare Part D prescription drug program and the Children's Health Insurance Program (CHIP). Medicare also funds the State Health Insurance Assistance Program (SHIP), which offers education and other assistance to Medicare beneficiaries and their families. These efforts differ in significant ways from current, ACA outreach efforts, but have similarities including broad public relations and advertising components and extensive use of trained volunteers and community groups to help consumers make decisions about health insurance. CMS officials have looked to the programs for lessons and guidance as they launch the in-person assistance programs.

In general, government and private sector analyses of the earlier HHS efforts indicate that the most effective outreach includes a variety of techniques including distributing information via mass media; cooperation between federal and state agencies, non-profit and business organizations; and the use of community groups and individual counseling to reach low-income consumers and those with language barriers or physical disabilities.

Medicare Part D

Congress approved the voluntary, Medicare Part D prescription drug program in the Medicare Modernization Act of 2003 (MMA, P.L. 108-173). Similar to the structure of the ACA, Part D enrollees may choose from a variety of private insurance plans. An estimated 42 million Medicare beneficiaries were eligible for the initial Part D benefit. The MMA also shifted dual eligible beneficiaries—individuals who qualify for both Medicare and Medicaid—to Part D from the Medicaid program. Medicare beneficiaries were eligible to apply for a transitional, temporary drug discount card program for 2004-2005, with the full Part D benefit taking effect on January 1, 2006.

Congress provided $1 billion to implement Medicare Part D.[108] According to a GAO audit of the program, HHS used about $99 million of the $1 billion for direct outreach and education activities, including $67.3 million for materials targeted at beneficiaries and $31.6 million for efforts to reach out to Medicare providers. For example, CMS paid the public relations firm Ketchum $47.3 million for outreach initiatives including a bus tour that targeted key cities to promote the prescription drug program.[109] Other CMS spending included more than $234 million to operate a 1-800 help line to answer questions about the Part D program, according to the GAO.

As part of the overall effort, HHS, the Social Security Administration (SSA), state Medicaid programs, and other entities implemented a coordinated education and outreach campaign, focusing on low-income beneficiaries.[110] The project included distributing more than 70 written publications, creating the toll-free help line, and posting information on the Medicare website. CMS worked with coalitions that included the National Alliance for Hispanic Health, the National Association of Area Agencies on Aging, the National Council on Aging, and the Pharmaceutical Research and Manufacturers Association.[111] The Regional Education about Choice in Health (REACH) program was aimed at beneficiaries with language, literacy, income, and other barriers to access,[112] while the Access to Benefits Coalition (ABC) was a group of nonprofits including AARP, the Salvation Army, and the American Hospital Association, and 56 local coalitions.[113] Pharmaceutical and insurance companies were active in outreach efforts, including the Medicare Rx Education Network.[114] CMS also worked through State Health Insurance and

Assistance Programs (see below) and increased funding to the SHIPs to help expand outreach.[115]

Even with the coordinated efforts, millions of eligible low-income individuals did not sign up for the drug discount card, and Medicare Part D enrollment was initially less than expected. However, by 2010, 90% of those eligible had Part D drug coverage, retiree coverage subsidized by Medicare, or private coverage at least as comprehensive as the Part D benefit.[116] More than 30 million beneficiaries were enrolled in Part D plans in 2013.

State Health Insurance and Assistance Programs (SHIP)

The State Health Insurance and Assistance Program (SHIP) provides counseling and information assistance to Medicare beneficiaries and their families regarding Medicare and other health insurance issues. The SHIP is authorized under Section 4360 of the Omnibus Budget Reconciliation Act of 1990 (P.L. 101-508). Although the program's authorization of appropriations expired in FY1996, Congress continues to provide funding by transferring discretionary funding to the program from the Federal Hospital Insurance Trust Fund and the Federal Supplementary Medical Insurance Trust Fund.

Paid and volunteer SHIP counselors provide one-on-one services to Medicare beneficiaries, both in person and by telephone. There are SHIP offices in all 50 states, as well as the District of Columbia, Guam, Puerto Rico, and the Virgin Islands. Of the 54 SHIP grant programs, about two- thirds are administered by State Units on Aging established under the Older Americans Act (OAA extended by the OAA Extension of 2006, P.L. 109-365).

The more than 15,000 counselors at the 1,300 local SHIP sites serve more than 5 million consumers annually.[117]

State SHIP programs provide training for volunteers, whose duties include answering questions about Medicare, Medigap supplemental insurance, Medicare Part C, Medicare Part D, and low- income subsidies. CMS, as part of its grant making, requires SHIPs to demonstrate how their training and certification programs will ensure that counselors provide accurate information. CMS provides materials for use in creating state certification programs, and analyzes SHIP performance each year.[118] According to a recent survey of SHIP offices, initial counselor training averages 20.5 hours, and about 75% of the programs require counselors to pass a certification test.[119] CMS runs a National Medicare Training Program that assists SHIP and other volunteers.

Children's Health Insurance Program

The State Children's Health Insurance Program (CHIP) was established in the Balanced Budget Act of 1997 (BBA 97; P.L. 105-33).[120] The law was reauthorized in The Children's Health Insurance Program Reauthorization Act of 2009 (CHIPRA, P.L. 111-3). In general, CHIP allows states to cover targeted, low-income children in families with no insurance and incomes above state Medicaid limits.[121]

The BBA 97 allowed states to spend up to 10% of their initial CHIP benefit spending on administrative costs, including outreach (as opposed to 10% of the CHIP annual appropriated level). The law also permitted additional flexibility for states that expanded their Medicaid programs under CHIP. In this case, states were allowed to claim federal financial participation for administrative costs under either Medicaid or CHIP. In the Consolidated Appropriations Act of 2001 (P.L. 106-554), Congress permitted states to use up to 10% of their unspent FY1998 funds specifically for outreach activities. These outreach funds were above and beyond funding available under the existing 10% cap. There was also private funding to supplement the public outreach efforts, including funding from the Robert Wood Johnson Foundation.

Enrollment efforts included hiring outreach workers, ranging from welfare recipients to professionals and community groups, and distributing advertising and informational materials. As was the case with Part D, HHS and state Medicaid agencies worked with community groups, health care providers, and schools to contact potential beneficiaries.[122] According to the GAO, enrollment began slowly but picked up. By the end of 2000, about three years after the law was enacted, all states had implemented their programs.

Federal agencies, including the SSA and the Departments of Agriculture, the Interior, Education, HHS, Housing and Urban Development, Labor, and the Treasury, were involved in outreach efforts. As the program progressed, states found that one-on-one efforts with community and other groups became more important in terms of connecting with hard-to-reach groups, such as immigrants and people with limited English skills.[123] States worked with an array of groups, including religious organizations, chambers of commerce, private businesses, community health centers, and education organizations not just for outreach, but to help families fill out enrollment forms and submit applications.[124] States also simplified enrollment forms, coordinated data with their Medicaid programs, and increased their use of technology to speed up the process.

CHIPRA built on this system and authorized up to $100 million in outreach and enrollment grants for fiscal years 2009 through 2013. The bulk of the authorized funds, 80%, were to be allocated to states and community-based organizations for outreach campaigns focusing on rural areas and underserved populations. The ACA expands the time period for the CHIPRA outreach and enrollment grants through 2015 and increases the appropriation level to $140 million for FY2009- FY2015.

There are some significant differences between initial CHIP enrollment and the exchange outreach effort. The scope of the CHIP target population is far smaller than the potential exchange population. In addition, the CHIP statute was not prescriptive in terms of telling states how to meet screening and enrollment requirements to determine eligibility for Medicaid and/or CHIP. States had an incentive to enroll children in CHIP, because the states were eligible for enhanced federal matching funds to expand coverage to low-income uninsured women and children, without necessarily expanding their Medicaid programs.

OUTSTANDING ISSUES

Some lawmakers have raised questions and concerns about the navigator programs. Two subcommittees of the House Committee on Oversight and Investigations in May 2013 held a joint hearing on implementation of the navigator program.[125]

Adequacy of Privacy Protections

Some Members of Congress, state legislators, health care advocacy groups, and brokers and agents have raised questions about whether CMS regulations go far enough to ensure protection of enrollees' personal information, such as Social Security numbers.

Lawmakers have asked HHS for additional information about how much access navigators, non- navigators, and certified application counselors will have to enrollees' personal information.[126] Lawmakers have asked to see specific training materials and have sought information regarding handling of documents and potential background checks of navigator personnel. A group of 13 attorneys general in an August 14, 2013 letter also raised concerns about the privacy regulations.[127]

In an effort to strengthen privacy protections, HHS in May 2014 final rules required that navigators, non-navigators, and certified application counselors obtain authorization from a consumer before accessing his or her personally identifiable information, and maintain a record of the authorization. Consumers have a right to revoke the authorization at any time.[128]

The potential for privacy violations and other consumer swindles extends well beyond exchange- sanctioned consumer assistance programs, however. The Federal Trade Commission warned consumers in 2012 about scam artists seeking to obtain personal information under the guise of verifying information regarding ACA coverage.[129]

APPENDIX. CMS EXCHANGE PRIVACY REQUIREMENTS

45 CFR § 155.260 Privacy and Security of Personally Identifiable Information

(a) Creation, collection, use and disclosure.

(1) Where the Exchange creates or collects personally identifiable information for the purposes of determining eligibility for enrollment in a qualified health plan; determining eligibility for other insurance affordability programs, as defined in 155.20; or determining eligibility for exemptions from the individual responsibility provisions in section 5000A of the Code, the Exchange may only use or disclose such personally identifiable information to the extent such information is necessary to carry out the functions described in § 155.200 of this subpart.

(2) The Exchange may not create, collect, use, or disclose personally identifiable information while the Exchange is fulfilling its responsibilities in accordance with § 155.200 of this subpart unless the creation, collection, use, or disclosure is consistent with this section.

(3) The Exchange must establish and implement privacy and security standards that are consistent with the following principles:

(i) *Individual access.* Individuals should be provided with a simple and timely means to access and obtain their personally identifiable information in a readable form and format;

(ii) *Correction.* Individuals should be provided with a timely means to dispute the accuracy or integrity of their personally identifiable information and to have erroneous information corrected or to have a dispute documented if their requests are denied;

(iii) *Openness and transparency.* There should be openness and transparency about policies, procedures, and technologies that directly affect individuals and/or their personally identifiable information;

(iv) *Individual choice.* Individuals should be provided a reasonable opportunity and capability to make informed decisions about the collection, use, and disclosure of their personally identifiable information;

(v) *Collection, use, and disclosure limitations.* Personally identifiable information should be created, collected, used, and/or disclosed only to the extent necessary to accomplish a specified purpose(s) and never to discriminate inappropriately;

(vi) *Data quality and integrity.* Persons and entities should take reasonable steps to ensure that personally identifiable information is complete, accurate, and up-to-date to the extent necessary for the person's or entity's intended purposes and has not been altered or destroyed in an unauthorized manner;

(vii) *Safeguards.* Personally identifiable information should be protected with reasonable operational, administrative, technical, and physical safeguards to ensure its confidentiality, integrity, and availability and to prevent unauthorized or inappropriate access, use, or disclosure; and,

(viii) *Accountability.* These principles should be implemented, and adherence assured, through appropriate monitoring and other means and methods should be in place to report and mitigate non-adherence and breaches.

(4) For the purposes of implementing the principle described in paragraph (a)(3)(vii) of this section, the Exchange must establish and implement operational, technical, administrative and physical safeguards that are consistent with any applicable laws (including this section) to ensure—

(i) The confidentiality, integrity, and availability of personally identifiable information created, collected, used, and/or disclosed by the Exchange;
(ii) Personally identifiable information is only used by or disclosed to those authorized to receive or view it;
(iii) Return information, as such term is defined by section 6103(b)(2) of the Code, is kept confidential under section 6103 of the Code;
(iv) Personally identifiable information is protected against any reasonably anticipated threats or hazards to the confidentiality, integrity, and availability of such information;
(v) Personally identifiable information is protected against any reasonably anticipated uses or disclosures of such information that are not permitted or required by law; and
(vi) Personally identifiable information is securely destroyed or disposed of in an appropriate and reasonable manner and in accordance with retention schedules;

(5) The Exchange must monitor, periodically assess, and update the security controls and related system risks to ensure the continued effectiveness of those controls.
(6) The Exchange must develop and utilize secure electronic interfaces when sharing personally identifiable information electronically.

(b) Application to non-Exchange entities. Except for tax return information, which is governed by section 6103 of the Code, when collection, use or disclosure is not otherwise required by law, an Exchange must require the same or more stringent privacy and security standards (as § 155.260(a)) as a condition of contract or agreement with individuals or entities, such as Navigators, agents, and brokers, that:

(1) Gain access to personally identifiable information submitted to an Exchange; or
(2) Collect, use or disclose personally identifiable information gathered directly from applicants, qualified individuals, or enrollees while that individual or entity is performing the functions outlined in the agreement with the Exchange.

(c) *Workforce compliance*. The Exchange must ensure its workforce complies with the policies and procedures developed and implemented by the Exchange to comply with this section.

(d) *Written policies and procedures*. Policies and procedures regarding the creation collection, use, and disclosure of personally identifiable information must, at minimum:

(1) Be in writing, and available to the Secretary of HHS upon request; and

(2) Identify applicable law governing collection, use, and disclosure of personally identifiable information.

(e) *Data sharing*. Data matching and sharing arrangements that facilitate the sharing of personally identifiable information between the Exchange and agencies administering Medicaid, CHIP or the BHP for the exchange of eligibility information must:

(1) Meet any applicable requirements described in this section;

(2) Meet any applicable requirements described in section 1413(c)(1) and (c)(2) of the Affordable Care Act;

(3) Be equal to or more stringent than the requirements for Medicaid programs under section 1942 of the Act; and

(4) For those matching agreements that meet the definition of "matching program" under 5 U.S.C. 552a(a)(8), comply with 5 U.S.C. 552a(o).

(f) *Compliance with the Code*. Return information, as defined in section 6103(b)(2) of the Code, must be kept confidential and disclosed, used, and maintained only in accordance with section 6103 of the Code.

(g) *Improper use and disclosure of information*. Any person who knowingly and willfully uses or discloses information in violation of section 1411(g) of the Affordable Care Act will be subject to a civil penalty of not more than $25,000 per person or entity, per use or disclosure, in addition to other penalties that may be prescribed by law.

End Notes

[1] CRS Report R43066, *Federal Funding for Health Insurance Exchanges*, by Annie L. Mach and C. Stephen Redhead.

[2] Ibid. To qualify to use an exchange, an individual must be a citizen, national, or noncitizen who is lawfully present in the United States; must not be incarcerated, other than pending the disposition of charges; and must meet applicable state residency standards.

[3] Qualified health plans must meet ACA guidelines regarding benefits, cost-sharing and other features. Exchanges use a single application to determine eligibility for enrollment in QHPs, for federal assistance and government programs such as Medicaid, and the Children's Health Insurance Program (CHIP).

[4] CRS Report R41137, *Health Insurance Premium Credits in the Patient Protection and Affordable Care Act (ACA)*, by Bernadette Fernandez.

[5] CRS Report R41158, *Summary of Small Business Health Insurance Tax Credit Under the Patient Protection and Affordable Care Act (ACA)*, by Annie L. Mach.

[6] Congressional Budget Office, *Updated Estimates of the Effects of the Insurance Coverage Provisions of the Affordable Care Act*, Table 2, April 2014, http://www.cbo.gov/sites/default/files/cbofiles/attachments/45231- ACA_Estimates.pdf.

[7] Testimony of Gary Cohen, Deputy Administrator and Director, Center for Consumer Information and Insurance Oversight, Centers for Medicare & Medicaid Services, House Committee on Oversight and Government Reform, May 21, 2013, http://oversight.house.gov/wp-content/uploads/2013/05/Cohen-Testimony-Final.pdf, and U.S. Census Bureau, http://www.census.gov/hhes/www/hlthins/ data/incpovhlth/2011/ Table7.pdf.

[8] Navigator program regulations can be found at 45 C.F.R. Part 155.210; http://www.ecfr.gov/cgi-bin/retrieveECFR?gp=1&SID=8614bcc3938647b1f40def8fc1076542&ty=HTML&h=L&r= PART&n=45y1.0.1.2.70#45:1.0.1.2.70.3.27.3. Published *Federal Register* proposals and rules include: Department of Health and Human Services, "Patient Protection and Affordable Care Act; Establishment of Exchanges and Qualified Health Plans; Proposed Rule," 45 C.F.R. Parts 144 and 145, July 15, 2011, http://www.gpo.gov/fdsys/pkg/FR-2011-07-15/pdf/2011-17610.pdf; Department of Health and Human Services, "Patient Protection and Affordable Care Act; Establishment of Exchanges and Qualified Health Plans; Exchange Standards for Employers; Final Rule and Interim Final Rule," 45 C.F.R. Parts 155, 156, and 157, March 27, 2012, http://www.gpo.gov/fdsys/pkg/FR-2012-03-27/pdf/2012-6125.pdf; Centers for Medicare & Medicaid Services, "Patient Protection and Affordable Care Act; Exchange Functions: Standards for Navigators and Non-Navigator Assistance Personnel, Proposed Rule,"45 C.F.R. Part 155, April 5, 2013, https://federalregister.gov/a/2013-07951.pdf; Centers for Medicare & Medicaid Services, "Patient Protection and Affordable Care Act; Program Integrity: Exchange, SHOP, Premium Stabilization Programs, and Market Standards; Proposed Rule," 45 C.F.R. Parts 144, 147, 153, et al., June 19, 2013, http://www.gpo.gov/fdsys/pkg/FR-2013-06-19/pdf/2013-14540.pdf; Centers for Medicare & Medicaid Services, "Patient Protection and Affordable Care Act; Centers for Medicare & Medicaid Services, "Children's Health Insurance Programs, and Exchanges: Essential Health Benefits in Alternative Benefit Plans, Eligibility Notices, Fair Hearing and Appeal Processes for Medicaid and Exchange Eligibility Appeals and Other Provisions Related to Eligibility and Enrollment for Exchanges, Medicaid and CHIP, and Medicaid Premiums and Cost Sharing, Final Rule," 42 C.F.R. Parts 430, 431, 433,et al., 45 C.F.R. Part 155, pp. 42159-42322, July 15, 2013, http://www.gpo.gov/fdsys/pkg/FR-2013-07-15/pdf/2013-16271.pdf; Centers for Medicare & Medicaid Services, "Patient Protection and Affordable Care Act; Exchange Functions: Standards for Navigators and Non-Navigator Assistance Personnel, Consumer Assistance Tools and Programs of an Exchange and Certified Application Counselors, Final Rule,"45 C.F.R. Part 155, July 17, 2013, http://www.gpo.gov/ fdsys/pkg/FR-2013-07-17/pdf/2013-17125.pdf; and Centers for Medicare & Medicaid Services, "Patient Protection and Affordable Care Act; Program Integrity: Exchange, SHOP, and Eligibility Appeals; Final Rule," 45 C.F.R. Parts 147, 153, 155. et al., August 30, 2013, http://www.gpo.gov/fdsys/pkg/FR-2013-08-30/pdf/2013-21338.pdf; and Centers for Medicare & Medicaid Services, Patient Protection and Affordable Care Act; Exchange and Insurance Market for 2015 and Beyond; Final Rule," 45 C.F.R. Parts 144, 146, 147, May 27, 2014, http://www.gpo.gov/fdsys/pkg/FR-2014-05-27/ pdf/2014-11657.pdf.

[9] ACA, Section 1311.

[10] 45 C.F.R. 155.205(d) and (e) provide that each Exchange must conduct consumer assistance, outreach, and education activities, including the navigator program. According to CMS, establishing a non-Navigator consumer assistance program pursuant to 155.205(d) and (e) will help ensure that an exchange is reaching as broad a range of consumers as possible. See also Centers for Medicare & Medicaid Services, "Patient Protection and Affordable Care Act; Exchange Functions: Standards for Navigators and Non-Navigator Assistance Personnel, Consumer Assistance Tools and Programs of an Exchange and Certified Application Counselors, Final Rule," 45 C.F.R. Part 155, *Federal Register*, July 17, 2013, http://www.gpo.gov/fdsys/pkg/FR-2013-07-17/pdf/2013-17125.pdf.

[11] Centers for Medicare & Medicaid Services, "Helping Consumers Apply & Enroll Through the Marketplace," July 2013, http://www.cms.gov/CCIIO/Resources/Files/Downloads/ market place-ways-to-help.pdf.

[12] 45 C.F.R. 155.225.

[13] 45 C.F.R. 155.220. See also Department of Health and Human Services, Center for Consumer Information and Insurance Oversight, "Role of Agents, Brokers, and Web-Brokers in Health Insurance Marketplaces," May 1, 2013, http://www.healthreformgps.org/wp-content/uploads/agent-broker-5-2.pdf.

[14] Centers for Medicare & Medicaid Services, "Patient Protection and Affordable Care Act; Program Integrity: Exchange, SHOP, and Eligibility Appeals; Final Rule,", 45 C.F.R. Parts 147, 153, 155. et al., *Federal Register*, August 30, 2013, http://www.gpo.gov/fdsys/pkg/FR-2013-08-30/pdf/2013-21338.pdf.

[15] *Associated Press*, "Missouri Governor Vetoes Health Navigator Limits," July 8, 2014, http://www.modernhealthcare.com/article/20140708/INFO/307089976.

[16] Centers for Medicare & Medicaid Services, "Patient Protection and Affordable Care Act; Exchange Functions: Standards for Navigators and Non-Navigator Assistance Personnel, Consumer Assistance Tools and Programs of an Exchange and Certified Application Counselors, Final Rule," 45 C.F.R. Part 155, *Federal Register*, p. 42831, July 17, 2013, http://www.gpo.gov/fdsys/pkg/FR-2013-07-17/pdf/2013-17125.pdf; and Centers for Medicare & Medicaid Services, Patient Protection and Affordable Care Act; Exchange and Insurance Market for 2015 and Beyond; Final Rule," 45 C.F.R. Parts 144, 146, 147, Federal Register, May 27, 2014, http://www.gpo.gov/fdsys/pkg/FR-2014-05-27/ pdf/2014-11657. pdf.

[17] Centers for Medicare & Medicaid Services, "Patient Protection and Affordable Care Act; Exchange Functions: Standards for Navigators and Non-Navigator Assistance Personnel," 45 C.F.R. Part 155, *Federal Register*, p. 20583, April 5, 2013, https://federalregister.gov/ a/2013-07951. The exchanges verify information regarding citizenship or immigration status, residency, income, and other factors affecting enrollee eligibility. In certain cases agents and insurance firms may enroll individuals "as through an exchange."

[18] ACA, Section 1311, http://www.gpo.gov/fdsys/pkg/BILLS-111hr3590enr/pdf/BILLS-111hr 3590enr.pdf.

[19] 45 C.F.R. 155.210(c)(2). See Department of Health and Human Services, "Patient Protection and Affordable Care Act; Establishment of Exchanges and Qualified Health Plans; Exchange Standards for Employers; Final Rule and Interim Final Rule," 45 C.F.R. Parts 155, 156, and 157, *Federal Register*, March 27, 2012, p. 18332, http://www.gpo.gov/ fdsys/pkg/FR-2012-03-27/pdf/2012-6125.pdf.

[20] 45 C.F.R. 155.215. See Centers for Medicare & Medicaid Services, "Patient Protection and Affordable Care Act; Exchange Functions: Standards for Navigators and Non-Navigator Assistance Personnel, Consumer Assistance Tools and Programs of an Exchange and Certified Application Counselors, Final Rule," 45 C.F.R. Part 155, Federal Register, pp. 42831-42833, July 17, 2013, http://www.gpo.gov/fdsys/pkg/FR-2013-07-17/pdf/2013-17125.pdf. Consideration is defined to include any monetary or nonmonetary commission, kick-back, salary, hourly wage or payment made directly or indirectly to the entity or

individual from an insurance company. Examples could include free travel, gifts or other items for steering consumers to a particular health plan.

[21] Centers for Medicare & Medicaid Services, "Patient Protection and Affordable Care Act; Exchange Functions: Standards for Navigators and Non-Navigator Assistance Personnel, Consumer Assistance Tools and Programs of an Exchange and Certified Application Counselors, Final Rule," 45 C.F.R. Part 155, *Federal Register*, July 17, 2013, pp. 42831-42833, http://www.gpo.gov/fdsys/pkg/FR-2013-07-17/pdf/2013-17125.pdf.

[22] Ibid. The rules bar an issuer of stop-loss insurance, a subsidiary of a stop-loss company, or an individual or entity that receives direct or indirect consideration from a stop-loss insurer for enrolling people in health insurance plans. CMS says that a navigator should not have a personal interest in whether a small employer chooses to self-insure its employees, or chooses to enroll in fully funded insurance coverage inside or outside an exchange.

[23] Centers for Medicare & Medicaid Services, Patient Protection and Affordable Care Act; Exchange and Insurance Market for 2015 and Beyond; Final Rule," 45 C.F.R. Parts 144, 146, 147, *Federal Register*, May 27, 2014, http://www.gpo.gov/fdsys/pkg/FR-2014-05-27/pdf/2014-11657.pdf; and 45 C.F.R. 155.210(d)(4). The rules also to non-navigators and certified application counselors.

[24] Centers for Medicare & Medicaid Services, "Patient Protection and Affordable Care Act; Program Integrity: Exchange, SHOP, and Eligibility Appeals; Final Rule," 45 C.F.R. Parts 147, 153, 155. et al., *Federal Register*, August 30, 2013, p. 54117, http://www.gpo.gov/fdsys/pkg/FR-2013-08-30/pdf/2013-21338.pdf; and 45 C.F.R. 155.705(d).

[25] Centers for Medicare & Medicaid Services, "Patient Protection and Affordable Care Act; Exchange and Insurance Market for 2015 and Beyond; Final Rule," 45 C.F.R. Parts 144, 146, 147, Federal Register, May 27, 2014, http://www.gpo.gov/fdsys/pkg/FR-2014-05-27/pdf/2014-11657.pdf. See also 45 C.F.R. 155.210(e)(7).

[26] Centers for Medicare & Medicaid Services, Navigator Funding Application, "PPHF–2013–Cooperative Agreement to Support Navigators in Federally-facilitated and State Partnership Exchanges," April 9, 2013, http://apply07.grants.gov/apply/opportunities/instructions/oppCA-NAV-13-001-cfda93.750-cidCA-NAV-13-001-017645-instructions.pdf.

[27] Centers for Medicare & Medicaid Services, "New Resources Available to Help Consumers Navigate the Health Insurance Marketplace," August 15, 2013, http://www.cms.gov/Newsroom/MediaReleaseDatabase/Press-Releases/2013-Press-Releases-Items/2013-08-15.html.

[28] Centers for Medicare & Medicaid Services, "CMS Announces Opportunity to Apply for Navigator Grants in Federally-facilitated and State Partnership Marketplaces," June 10, 2014, http://www.cms.gov/Newsroom/ MediaReleaseDatabase/Press-releases/2014-Press-releases-items/2014-06-10.html; and Centers for Medicare &Medicaid Services, Center for Consumer Information and Insurance Oversight, "Cooperative Agreement to Support Navigators in Federally-facilitated and State Partnership Marketplaces," June 10, 2014.

[29] Ibid.

[30] Centers for Medicare &Medicaid Services, Center for Consumer Information and Insurance Oversight, "Cooperative Agreement to Support Navigators in Federally-facilitated and State Partnership Marketplaces," June 10, 2014, p. 28.

[31] For a discussion of non-navigator programs see Centers for Medicare & Medicaid Services, "Patient Protection and Affordable Care Act; Exchange Functions: Standards for Navigators and Non-Navigator Assistance Personnel, Proposed Rule," 45 C.F.R. Part 155, *Federal Register*, April 5, 2013, p. 20583, https://federalregister.gov/a/2013-07951.pdf; and Centers for Medicare & Medicaid Services, "Patient Protection and Affordable Care Act; Exchange Functions: Standards for Navigators and Non-Navigator Assistance Personnel, Consumer Assistance Tools and Programs of an Exchange and Certified Application Counselors, Final Rule," 45 C.F.R. Part 155, Federal Register, July 17, 2013, p. 42825, http://www.gpo.gov/fdsys/pkg/FR-2013-07-17/pdf/2013-17125.pdf.

[32] Ibid. In a consumer partnership exchange, a state is responsible for the day-to-day management of the exchange navigators and the development and management of a separate in-person assistance program, and can choose to be responsible for outreach and educational activities. HHS will operate the exchange call center and website and be responsible for the funding and award of navigator grants. Centers for Medicare & Medicaid Services, "Guidance on State Partnership Exchange," January 3, 2013, http://www.cms.gov/ CCIIO/Resources/Fact-Sheets-and-FAQs/ Downloads/partnership-guidance-01-03-2013.pdf. A partnership exchange is a second type of partnership. In this type of exchange, states assume primary plan management responsibility.

[33] Centers for Medicare & Medicaid Services, "Patient Protection and Affordable Care Act; Exchange Functions: Standards for Navigators and Non-Navigator Assistance Personnel, Consumer Assistance Tools and Programs of an Exchange and Certified Application Counselors, Final Rule," 45 C.F.R. Part 155, *Federal Register*, p. 42825, July 17, 2013, http://www.gpo.gov/fdsys/pkg/FR-2013-07-17/pdf/2013-17125.pdf.

[34] A state-run exchange may set up or continue to operate a non-navigator program from its own funds after its first year of operation to supplement its fully funded navigator program.

[35] CRS Report R43066, *Federal Funding for Health Insurance Exchanges*, by Annie L. Mach and C. Stephen Redhead.

[36] 45 C.F.R. 155.215. See also Centers for Medicare & Medicaid Services, "Patient Protection and Affordable Care Act; Exchange Functions: Standards for Navigators and Non-Navigator Assistance Personnel, Consumer Assistance Tools and Programs of an Exchange and Certified Application Counselors, Final Rule," 45 C.F.R. Part 155, *Federal Register*, July 17, 2013, http://www.gpo.gov/fdsys/pkg/FR-2013-07-17/pdf/2013-17125.pdf. Non-navigator programs are also called in-person assistance programs.

[37] 45 C.F.R. 155.215(h).

[38] Kaiser Family Foundation, "Navigator and In-Person Assistance Programs: A Snapshot of State Programs," April 2013, http://kaiserfamilyfoundation.files.wordpress.com/ 2013/ 04/8437.pdf.

[39] 45 C.F.R. 155.225, Centers for Medicare & Medicaid Services, "Patient Protection and Affordable Care Act; Exchange Functions: Standards for Navigators and Non-Navigator Assistance Personnel, Consumer Assistance Tools and Programs of an Exchange and Certified Application Counselors, Final Rule," 45 C.F.R. Part 155, Federal Register, p. 42824 and 42828, July 17, 2013, http://www.gpo.gov/fdsys/pkg/FR-2013-07-17/pdf/2013-17125.pdf. Helping to facilitate enrollment means helping consumers with application forms, clarifying differences among QHPs, and helping a qualified individual decide on a plan.

[40] Ibid.

[41] Centers for Medicare & Medicaid Services, "Guidance on Certified Application Counselor Program for the Federally-Facilitated Marketplace including State Partnership Marketplaces," July 12, 2013, http://www.cms.gov/ CCIIO/Resources/Regulations-and-Guidance/Downloads/CAC-guidance-7-12-2013.pdf.

[42] Centers for Medicare & Medicaid Services, "Helping Consumers Apply & Enroll through the Marketplace," http://www.cms.gov/CCIIO/Resources/Files/Downloads/marketplace-ways-to-help.pdf.

[43] 45 C.F.R. Part 155.225 (c).

[44] Ibid.

[45] Centers for Medicare & Medicaid Services, "Patient Protection and Affordable Care Act; Exchange Functions: Standards for Navigators and Non-Navigator Assistance Personnel, Consumer Assistance Tools and Programs of an Exchange and Certified Application Counselors, Final Rule," 45 C.F.R. Part 155, *Federal Register*, July 17, 2013, p.42825, http://www.gpo.gov/fdsys/pkg/FR-2013-07-17/pdf/2013-17125.pdf. In addition, exchanges, rather than counselors, would refer enrollees to other state or federal programs, to help them with grievances or complaints regarding health coverage.

[46] 45 C.F.R. 155.225.
[47] 45 C.F.R. 155.225(g)(2).
[48] May 27 FR, p. 30323, C.F.R. 155.225.
[49] 45 C.F.R. 155.225(b)(3).
[50] Department of Health and Human Services, "Health Centers to Help Uninsured Individuals Gain Affordable Health Insurance Coverage," May 9, 2013, http://www.hhs.gov/news/press/2013pres/05/20130509a.html#.UgQP88q2rz4.
[51] Department of Health and Human Services, "Health Centers to Help Uninsured Americans Gain Affordable Health Insurance Coverage," December 11, 2013, http://www.hhs.gov/news/press/2013pres/12/20131211b.html.
[52] 45 C.F.R. 155.215, Centers for Medicare & Medicaid Services, "Patient Protection and Affordable Care Act; Exchange Functions: Standards for Navigators and Non-Navigator Assistance Personnel, Consumer Assistance Tools and Programs of an Exchange and Certified Application Counselors, Final Rule," 45 C.F.R. Part 155, *Federal Register*; July 17, 2013, p. 42833, http://www.gpo.gov/fdsys/pkg/FR-2013-07-17/pdf/2013-17125.pdf.
[53] Ibid.
[54] 45 C.F.R. 155.225(d)(2). Centers for Medicare & Medicaid Services, "Patient Protection and Affordable Care Act; Exchange Functions: Standards for Navigators and Non-Navigator Assistance Personnel, Consumer Assistance Tools and Programs of an Exchange and Certified Application Counselors, Final Rule," 45 C.F.R. Part 155, *Federal Register*, pp. 42825-42826, July 17, 2013, http://www.gpo.gov/fdsys/pkg/FR-2013-07-17/pdf/2013-17125.pdf.
[55] Assisters such as navigators and non-navigators are required to keep a record of the authorization. In a federally financed exchange, the record must be retained for a minimum of six years.
[56] Ibid, p. 6 and 45 C.F.R. 155.215.
[57] 45 C.F.R. 155.215(i) and 155.225(g)(3). The provision applies to federally funded exchanges. Assisters operating in SHOP exchanges are not subject to the rule, though CMS will evaluate and monitor the exchanges.
[58] 45 C.F.R. 155.210(d)(5), 155.215(a)(2)(i), and 155.225(g)(1).
[59] 45 C.F.R. 155.210(d)(6), 155.215(a)(2)(i), and 155.225(g)(4).
[60] Ibid.
[61] Ibid.
[62] 45 C.F.R. 155.420, Special enrollment periods.
[63] 45 C.F.R. 155.215(b) Centers for Medicare & Medicaid Services, "Patient Protection and Affordable Care Act; Exchange Functions: Standards for Navigators and Non-Navigator Assistance Personnel, Consumer Assistance Tools and Programs of an Exchange and Certified Application Counselors, Final Rule," 45 C.F.R. Part 155, *Federal Register*, July 17, 2013, http://www.gpo.gov/fdsys/pkg/FR-2013-07-17/pdf/2013-17125.pdf.
[64] Ibid, p. 42837.
[65] Centers for Medicare &Medicaid Services, Center for Consumer Information and Insurance Oversight, "Cooperative Agreement to Support Navigators in Federally-facilitated and State Partnership Marketplaces," June 10, 2014, p. 9.
[66] Department of Health and Human Services, "New Resources Available to Help Consumers Navigate the Health Insurance Marketplace," August 15, 2013, http://www.hhs.gov/news/press/2013pres/08/20130815a.html and HHS letter to Representative Fred Upton, September 9, 2013.
[67] Henry J. Kaiser Family Foundation, "Navigator and In-Person Assistance Programs: A Snapshot of State Programs," April 2013, http://www.healthexchange.ca.gov/ Board Meetings/Documents/April%2023,%202013/ Reports%20and%20Research%20-%20 Master_April.pdf#page=36.

[68] Centers for Medicare & Medicaid Services, *Health Insurance Marketplace Navigator Standard Operating Procedures Manual*, August 2013, http://www.healthreformgps.org/wp-content/uploads/navigator-SOP-manual-8-26.pdf.

[69] 45 C.F.R. 155.215 (c 1), and Centers for Medicare & Medicaid Services, Navigator Funding Application, "PPHF–2013–Cooperative Agreement to Support Navigators in Federally-facilitated and State Partnership Exchanges," April 9,2013, http://apply07.grants.gov/apply/opportunities/instructions/oppCA-NAV-13-001-cfda93.750-cidCA-NAV-13-001-017645-instructions.pdf.

[70] 45 C.F.R. 155.225 (d)(1), and Centers for Medicare & Medicaid Services, "Patient Protection and Affordable Care Act; Exchange Functions: Standards for Navigators and Non-Navigator Assistance Personnel, Consumer Assistance Tools and Programs of an Exchange and Certified Application Counselors, Final Rule," 45 C.F.R. Part 155, *Federal Register*, p. 42846, July 17, 2013, http://www.gpo.gov/fdsys/pkg/FR-2013-07-17/pdf/2013-17125.pdf.

[71] Tax return information is covered by Section 6103 of the IRS Code.

[72] Centers for Medicare & Medicaid Services, "Guidance on Certified Application Counselor Program for the Federally-Facilitated Marketplace including State Partnership Marketplaces," July 12, 2013, http://www.cms.gov/ CCIIO/Resources/Regulations-and-Guidance/Downloads/CAC-guidance-7-12-2013.pdf.

[73] Centers for Medicare & Medicaid Services, "Patient Protection and Affordable Care Act; Program Integrity: Exchange, SHOP, and Eligibility Appeals; Final Rule," 45 C.F.R. Parts 147, 153, 155. et al., *Federal Register*, August 30, 2013, p. 54080, http://www.gpo.gov/fdsys/pkg/FR-2013-08-30/pdf/2013-21338.pdf.

[74] Ibid and 45 C.F.R. 155.280.

[75] Ibid, p. 54084. While initial rules called for a security breach to be reported within an hour, CMS did not include the time limit in final rules. CMS noted that the one-hour incident response timeline has been included in all data-sharing agreements required under the ACA. According to CMS: "Because the one hour incident response timeline has been included in all the data sharing agreements required under the Affordable Care Act, we have deleted the timing for incident reporting from regulation, proposed in § 155.280(c)(3), and expect it to be addressed through separate agreement."

[76] 45 C.F.R. 155.210(c)(1)(iii), directs that, to receive a navigator grant, an entity or individual must ''meet any licensing, certification or other standards prescribed by the state or exchange, if applicable.''

[77] ACA, Section 1321(d). Centers for Medicare & Medicaid Services, "Patient Protection and Affordable Care Act; Exchange Functions: Standards for Navigators and Non-Navigator Assistance Personnel, Consumer Assistance Tools and Programs of an Exchange and Certified Application Counselors, Final Rule," 45 C.F.R. Part 155, *Federal Register*, July 17, 2013, http://www.gpo.gov/fdsys/pkg/FR-2013-07-17/pdf/2013-17125.pdf. CMS regulations state that holding an agent or broker license is neither necessary, nor by itself sufficient, to perform the duties of a navigator, because licenses generally do not address areas in which navigators need expertise, including public coverage options that would be available to some consumers.

[78] Ibid.

[79] 45 C.F.R. 155.210. CMS in July 2013 regulations had specified that states could not require navigators to carry errors and omission coverage, but replaced that language in May 2014 with a broader prohibition against any requirement that would in effect render all navigators in the exchange to be licensed agents and brokers. Centers for Medicare & Medicaid Services, "Patient Protection and Affordable Care Act; Exchange and Insurance Market for 2015 and Beyond; Final Rule," 45 C.F.R. Parts 144, 146, 147, *Federal Register*, May 27, 2014, p. 30322, http://www.gpo.gov/fdsys/pkg/FR-2014-05-27/pdf/2014-11657.pdf.

[80] Department of Health and Human Services, "Patient Protection and Affordable Care Act; Establishment of Exchanges and Qualified Health Plans; Exchange Standards for

Employers; Final Rule and Interim Final Rule," 45 C.F.R. Parts 155, 156, and 157, p. 18331, March 27, 2012, http://www.gpo.gov/fdsys/pkg/FR-2012-03-27/pdf/2012-6125.pdf.

[81] 45 C.F.R. 155.210(c)(2).

[82] Centers for Medicare & Medicaid Services, "Patient Protection and Affordable Care Act; Exchange and Insurance Market for 2015 and Beyond; Final Rule," 45 C.F.R. Parts 144, 146, 147, *Federal Register*, May 27, 2014, p. 30344, http://www.gpo.gov/fdsys/pkg/FR-2014-05-27/pdf/2014-11657.pdf.

[83] Regarding the first two bullets, navigators in state SHOP-only exchanges are permitted under federal law to fulfill some of their duties through referrals to agents and brokers, if state law allows.

[84] Centers for Medicare & Medicaid Services, Center for Consumer Information & Insurance Oversight, "Navigator Grant Awards" August 15, http://www.cms.gov/CCIIO/Programs-and-Initiatives/Health-Insurance-Marketplaces/ Downloads/navigator-list-8-15-2013.pdf; and Navigator Funding Application, "PPHF–2013–Cooperative Agreement to Support Navigators in Federally-facilitated and State Partnership Exchanges," April 9, 2013, http://apply07.grants.gov/ apply/opportunities/instructions/oppCA-NAV-13-001-cfda93.750-cidCA-NAV-13-001-017645-instructions.pdf. CMS also released a list of organizations and businesses working with HHS on outreach, in addition to other consumer assistance programs. See http://marketplace.cms.gov/help-us/champions-for-coverage-list.pdf.

[85] Ibid. p. 10. For example, a grant may end sooner than 12 months if a federally facilitated exchange or state partnership exchange is replaced by a state-based exchange. In addition, the ability of a grantee to receive quarterly funding installments depends on whether it is in compliance with the terms and conditions of the grant.

[86] Centers for Medicare & Medicaid Services, Center for Consumer Information and Insurance Oversight, "Cooperative Agreement to Support Navigators in Federally-facilitated and State Partnership Marketplaces," June 10, 2014.

[87] CRS Report R43066, *Federal Funding for Health Insurance Exchanges*, by Annie L. Mach and C. Stephen Redhead.

[88] Centers for Medicare & Medicaid Services, "Patient Protection and Affordable Care Act; Exchange Functions: Standards for Navigators and Non-Navigator Assistance Personnel, Consumer Assistance Tools and Programs of an Exchange and Certified Application Counselors, Final Rule," 45 C.F.R. Part 155, *Federal Register*, p. 42825, July 17, 2013, http://www.gpo.gov/fdsys/pkg/FR-2013-07-17/pdf/2013-17125.pdf.

[89] Federally facilitated and partnership exchanges may use Section 1311 funds for certain functions, including some administrative costs, as outlined by CMS. See "Frequently Asked Questions on Allowable Uses of Section 1311 Funding for States in a State Partnership Marketplace or in States with a Federally-Facilitated Marketplace," http://www.cms.gov/CCIIO/Resources/Fact-Sheets-and-FAQs/spm-ffm-funding.html.

[90] Ian Hill, Margaret Wilkinson, and Bridget Courtout, The Urban Institute, "The Launch of the Affordable Care Act in Selected States: Outreach, Education, and Enrollment Assistance," March 2014, Table 2, http://www.urban.org/ UploadedPDF/413039-The-Launch-of-the-Affordable-Care-Act-in-Eight-States-Outreach-Education-and-Enrollment- Assistance.pdf.

[91] Karen Pollitz, Jennifer Tolbert, and Rosa Ma, *Survey of Helath Insurance Marketplace Assister Programs*: A First Look at Consumer Assistance under the Affordable Care Act, Kaiser Family Foundation, July 2014, p. 11.

[92] CRS Report R41439, *Health Insurance Agents and Brokers in the Reformed Health Insurance Market*, by Bernadette Fernandez.

[93] U.S. Department of Labor, Bureau of Labor Standards, 2012 Occupational Outlook Handbook: Insurance Sales Agents, http://www.bls.gov/ooh/sales/insurance-sales-agents.htm#tab-1.

[94] The Dodd-Frank Wall Street Reform and Consumer Protection Act of 2010 (P.L. 111-203), expanded the federal regulatory role over other areas of the insurance industry. For more background, see CRS Report R43067, *Insurance Regulation: Issues, Background, and Legislation in the 113th Congress*, by Baird Webel.

[95] For more information on Medicare oversight of producers see Centers for Medicare and Medicaid Services, "Chapter 3 – Medicare Marketing Guidelines For Medicare Advantage Plans, Medicare Advantage Prescription Drug Plans, Prescription Drug Plans, and Section 1876 Cost Plans," June 17, 2014, http://www.cms.gov/Medicare/Health-Plans/ Managed CareMarketing/FinalPartCMarketingGuidelines.html.

[96]CRS Report R42735, *Medical Loss Ratio Requirements Under the Patient Protection and Affordable Care Act (ACA): Issues for Congress*, by Suzanne M. Kirchhoff.

[97] 45 C.F.R. 155.220. Centers for Medicare & Medicaid Services, "Patient Protection and Affordable Care Act; Establishment of Exchanges and Qualified Health Plans; Exchange Standards for Employers; Final Rule and Interim Final Rule," 45 C.F.R. Parts 155, 156, and 157, *Federal Register*, March 27, 2012, http://www.gpo.gov/fdsys/pkg/FR-2012-03-27/pdf/2012-6125.pdf; and HHS Center for Consumer Information and Insurance Oversight, "Role of Agents, Brokers, and Web-brokers in Health Insurance Marketplaces," May 1, 2013, http://www.healthreformgps.org/wp- content/uploads/agent-broker-5-2.pdf.

[98] Department of Health and Human Services, Center for Consumer Information and Insurance Oversight, "Role of Agents, Brokers, and Web-Brokers in Health Insurance Marketplaces," p. 6, May 1, 2013, http://www.healthreformgps.org/wp-content/uploads/agent-broker-5-2.pdf.

[99] Department of Health and Human Services, Center for Consumer Information and Insurance Oversight, "Role of Agents, Brokers, and Web-Brokers in Health Insurance Marketplaces," p. 5, May 1, 2013, http://www.healthreformgps.org/wp-content/uploads/agent-broker-5-2.pdf.

[100] Ibid.

[101] Centers for Medicare & Medicaid Services, "Federally-facilitated Marketplace: Agent/Broker Training Launch," August 2013, http://www.cms.gov/CCIIO/Programs-and-Initiatives/ Health-Insurance-Marketplaces/Downloads/agent- broker-training-webinar.pdf.

[102] Centers for Medicare & Medicaid Services, "Patient Protection and Affordable Care Act; Program Integrity: Exchange, SHOP, and Eligibility Appeals; Final Rule," 45 C.F.R. Parts 147, 153, 155. et al., *Federal Register*, August 30, 2013, http://www.gpo.gov/fdsys/pkg/FR-2013-08-30/pdf/2013-21338.pdf.

[103] 45 C.F.R. 155.220.

[104] Centers for Medicare & Medicaid Services, "Patient Protection and Affordable Care Act; Program Integrity: Exchange, SHOP, and Eligibility Appeals; Final Rule," 45 C.F.R. Parts 147, 153, 155. et al., *Federal Register*, August 30, 2013, p. 54078, http://www.gpo.gov/ fdsys/pkg/FR-2013-08-30/pdf/2013-21338.pdf, and HHS, Center for Consumer Information and Insurance Oversight, "Role of Agents, Brokers, and Web-Brokers in Health Insurance Marketplaces," May 1, 2013, http://www.healthreformgps.org/wp-content/uploads/agent-broker-5-2.pdf. Consumers may go to the federal website Healthcare.gov for background information about the insurance exchange system.

[105] C.F.R. 156.1230 and Centers for Medicare & Medicaid Services, "Patient Protection and Affordable Care Act; Program Integrity: Exchange, SHOP, and Eligibility Appeals; Final Rule," 45 C.F.R. Parts 147, 153, 155. et al., *Federal Register*, August 30, 2013, p. 54146, http://www.gpo.gov/fdsys/pkg/FR-2013-08-30/pdf/2013-21338.pdf.

[106] 45 C.F.R. 155.20 defines an issuer application assister as an employee, contractor, or agent of a QHP issuer who is not licensed as an agent, broker, or producer under state law and who assists individuals in the individual market with applying for a determination or redetermination of eligibility for coverage through the exchange or for insurance affordability programs

[107] Ibid.

[108] Department of Health and Human Services, *Fiscal 2006 Budget in Brief*, p. 56, http://archive.hhs.gov/budget/06budget/FY2006BudgetinBrief.pdf. Congress transferred $25 million of that total to the HHS Office of the Inspector General for oversight activities.

[109] Government Accountability Office, "Internal Control Deficiencies Resulted in Millions of Dollars of Questionable Contract Payments," GAO-08-54, November 2007, http:// www.gao.gov/new.items/d0854.pdf. The GAO review found nearly $90 million in questionable spending.

[110] Government Accountability Office, "Medicare: Quality of CMS Communications to Beneficiaries on the Prescription Drug Benefit Could Be Improved," GAO-06-715T, May 4, 2006, http://www.gpo.gov/fdsys/pkg/ GAOREPORTS-GAO-06-715T/html/ GAORE PORTS -GAO-06-715T.htm.

[111] Laura Summer, Ellen O'Brien, Patricia Nemore, and Katharine Hsiao, Commonwealth Fund, "Medicare Part D: State and Local Efforts to Assist Vulnerable Beneficiaries," May 2008, http://www.commonwealthfund.org/~/media/ Files/Publications/Issue%20Brief/2008/May/ Medicare%20Part%20D%20%20State%20and%20Local%20Efforts%20to%20Assist%20V ulnerable%20Beneficiaries/Summer_McarePartDstatelocalefforts_1126_ib%20pdf.

[112] Government Accountability Office, "Medicare: CMS's Beneficiary Education and Outreach Efforts for the Medicare Prescription Drug Discount Card and Transitional Assistance Program," GAO-06-139R, November 30, 2005, http://www.gao.gov/assets/ 100/ 93875.html/.

[113] Ibid.

[114] *Kaiser Health News*, "Insurers, National Organizations Launch Advertising Campaigns for Medicare Rx Drug Benefit," July 20, 2005, http://www.kaiserhealthnews.org/Daily-Reports/2005/July/20/dr00031514.aspx?p=1.

[115] HHS Secretary Michael Leavitt, *Report to Congress: Best Practices for Enrolling Low-Income Beneficiaries into the Medicare Prescription Drug Benefit Program*, 2009, http://www. cms.gov/Research-Statistics-Data-and-Systems/Statistics-Trends-and-Reports/Reports/downloads/Leavitt_RTC_Best_Practices_Enrolling_LI.pdf

[116] Shinobu Suzuki, "Status Report on Part D," Medicare Payment Advisory Commission," January 11, 2013, http://www.medpac.gov/transcripts/status% 20report%20on%20part% 20D%20for%20jan%202013.pdf.

[117] Centers for Medicare & Medicaid Services, "Affordable Care Act State Health Insurance Assistance Program (SHIP) and Aging and Disability Resource Center (ADRC) Options Counseling for Medicare - Medicaid Individuals in States with Approved Financial Alignment Models," August 23, 2012, http://aoa.gov/AoARoot/Grants/Funding/docs/ 2012/SHIP_ADRC_Duals_FOA_FINAL8_22_2012.pdf.

[118] Centers for Medicare & Medicaid Services, National SHIP Resource Center, "Evaluating Your SHIP Training and Certification Program Toolkit," August 2012, https://www. shiptalk.org/ShipTalkInfoLib/MiscDocs/ OCCT_Eval_Webinar_Toolkit.pdf.

[119] Tobi Johnson and Lee Thompson, The National SHIP Resource Center, "SHIP Counselor Training and Certification Programs: Findings from a National Survey," January 2013, https://www.shiptalk.org/ShipTalkInfoLib/MiscDocs/SHIP_Training_Cert_Survey_508.pdf . The survey was distributed to the 54 state SHIP offices. Of that total, 85% answered the survey.

[120] CRS Report R40226, P.L. 111-3: *The Children's Health Insurance Program Reauthorization Act of 2009*, by Evelyne P. Baumrucker, Elicia J. Herz, and Jane G. Gravelle.

[121] Government Accountability Office, "Pre-Existing Condition Insurance Plan: Comparison of Implementation and Early Enrollment with the Children's Health Insurance Program," November 10, 2011, http://www.gao.gov/assets/590/586867.pdf. CHIP defined a targeted, low-income child as one who is under 19 years of age, with no health insurance, and who would not have been eligible for Medicaid under the rules in effect in the state on March 31, 1997.

[122] National Health Policy Forum, "CHIP and Medicaid Outreach and Enrollment: A Hands-On Look at Marketing and Applications," October 19, 1999, http://www.nhpf.org/library/issue-briefs/IB748_SCHIPOutreach_10-19-99.pdf.

[123] Susan Williams and Margo Rosenbach, Mathematica, "Evolution of State Outreach Efforts under SCHIP," *Health Care Financing Review*, Summer 2007, pp. 95-107, http://www. mathematica-mpr.com/publications/pdfs/ evolutionstate.pdf

[124] Victoria Wachino and Alice Weiss, "Maximizing Kids' Enrollment in Medicaid and SCHIP," National Academy for State Health Policy, February 2009, http://nashp.org/ sites/ default/files/Max_Enroll_Report_FINAL.pdf?q=files/ Max_Enroll_Report_FINAL. pdf.

[125] House Committee on Oversight and Government Reform, Subcommittee on Energy Policy, Health Care and Entitlements Subcommittee on Economic Growth, Job Creation and Regulatory Affairs, "Examining the Concerns about the ObamaCare Outreach Campaign Program," May 21, 2013, http://oversight.house.gov/hearing/examining-theconcerns-about-obamacare-outreach-campaign/.

[126] Letter to HHS Secretary Kathleen Sebelius, May 2013, http://waysandmeans.house.gov/ uploadedfiles/brady_boustany_navigator_letter_051513.pdf.

[127] Patrick Morrissey, West Virginia Attorney General, Letter to HHS Secretary Sebelius, August 14, 2013, http://www.wvago.gov/pdf/Letter%20to%20HHS%20re%20Data%20Privacy_%28final%208%2014%2013%29.pdf.

[128] 45 C.F.R. 155.210 (e) (6), 155 215.(g), and 155.225(f). See Centers for Medicare & Medicaid Services, "Patient Protection and Affordable Care Act; Exchange and Insurance Market for 2015 and Beyond; Final Rule," 45 C.F.R. Parts 144, 146, 147, *Federal Register*, May 27, 2014, http://www.gpo.gov/fdsys/pkg/FR-2014-05-27/pdf/2014-11657.pdf.

[129] Federal Trade Commission, "FTC Alert: Scammers Out to Trick Consumers Using the Supreme Court's Affordable Care Act Ruling," July 31, 2012, http://www.ftc.gov/ opa/2012/07/aca.shtm; Sid Kirchheimer, "New Health Benefits Scam,"AARP, March 13, 2013, http://www.aarp.org/money/scams-fraud/info-07-2012/affordable-care-act-scam.html; and Herb Weisbaum, "Beware of Obamacare Scammers," CNBC and The Fiscal Times, August 15, 2013, http://www. thefiscaltimes.com/Articles/2013/08/15/Beware-of-Obamacare-Scammers.aspx#page1.

INDEX

D

E

F

G

H

Q

S

T

U

V

W